For unto us a Child is born, unto us a
Son is given:
and the government shall be upon His
shoulder:
and His name shall be called
Wonderful,
Counsellor,
The Mighty God,
The Everlasting Father
The Prince of Peace.
Of the increase of His government and
peace
there shall be no end.

Isaiah 9:6-7

β

Table of Contents

|nauguration

Citizens of Columbia†[01] were outraged; new found evidence proved Nine Eleven was not a conspiracy theory, but veritably a conspiracy. Soldiers in historic propositions began to speak out about task force missions not associated with fighting terrorism: Generals discovered through reliable resources that Nine Eleven was nothing less than a plot to birth a New World Order; in result many Generals induced the general public's awareness through the World Wide Web. As Americans envisioned loved ones jump from a Twin Tower for dear life, chagrin channeled into revolution. Thence citizens of all nationalities and social classes protested by the thousands refusing to work, buy, or sell.

In order to keep the majority bewildered, mass media that once informed the world about unconstitutional government proceedings was limited to the internet; the avoidance of reporting governmental awareness was also due to the news broadcaster's fear of the National Defense Act causing termination—According to the National Defense Act any news broadcast resulting in belligerent acts involving American citizens was prohibited. The World Wide Web is also threatened as the Kill the Internet Bill reached the Supreme Court. In the meantime, truth about Nine Eleven spread through websites like wildfire, and protesters from every state began to amass. As residents of Washington District of Columbia, and the states, heard the truth, revolutionist gathered, and the destination was the White House.

Belial Fulgurite [*foo* l-grit], Commander in Chief, received word of the approaching protest and immediately held

01. The United States

any chaos in abeyance. Martial Law became reality as soldiers were ordered to enforce the National Defense Act, allowing scrutiny on every activist, placing them on the Most Likely to Create a Belligerent Act List. Many citizens resisted the search labeling it unconstitutional, but any refusal resulted in resisting arrest and many protestors were incarcerated.

Since television broadcasters were limited to only discuss weather, nature, entertainment, and foreign affairs; the average John/Jane Q. Public was not aware of the current events in America. Following the Supreme Court's ruling on the Kill the Internet Bill, demand for the World Wide Web was like gold after dollar flop, and due to abnormal interest in the Internet, web providers were forced to limit customers to Three Gigabytes per month with unreasonable overage cost. Any website partaking in reporting current events were marked with a colossal Gigabyte symbol, turning the average surfer away from the site, and all consumers "fortunate" enough to afford the overage were implanted with a RFID chip for surveillance.

Wars concerning other countries were still a part of everyday news, and rumors of attacks against the Columbia circulated ceaselessly. According to news reports, terrorism was at a quote unquote all-time high, also causing rumors of war amongst other counties; therefore most votes supported the National Defense Act, not aware of its essence. Researching any information about the National Defense Act was forbidden to supposedly limit any terrorist of obtaining the document. As groups protested the right to conceal information within the National Defense Act; they were secretly silenced. All Generals who spoke about Nine Eleven were discharged, placed on the Most Likely to Create a Belligerent Act List, and were convicted of Home Terrorism under the Homegrown Terrorism Prevention Act.

All discharged Generals were replaced by their Privates. Since Privates were willing to make sacrifices in order become the Generals who were once over them, the Privates' loyalty was tested similar to street gang initiations. Privates from other countries also participated in the initiations as well; they were kept on "tight observation" but many soldiers were even old members of the Taliban and Al-Qaida. The initiation gang became known as The Abeyance, and reports over the Internet of their disturbing initiations were simply smoke screened.

Tempered change in commerce and mass media seemed strange, but Belial kept Columbia entertained as the price of cable television, and Ticketmaster dropped dramatically. Deals were made by the Belial administration with taxpayer's money to compensate cable companies and Ticketmaster for the loss of revenue. There was a concert every weekend followed by an after party in every state. Superstars threw unforgettable jollifications on chest board designed floors accompanied by their male and/or female partner, one on the left shoulder and the other on the right; moreover homosexual partners were greatly appreciated and highly recommended to attend. Belial was up for election the coming year with one of his new slogans "Life is short, celebrate it." Since entertainment was in high demand, media stores were constructed in abundance. Due to the appalling economy as a result of Nine Eleven, citizens applauded the opening of the media stores and saw it as the change Belial promised when first taken office. The Belial administration had every strategy in process to accomplish an election for the history books moving towards a New World Order; unbeknownst to them the coming election would go down in history but will have an opposing result.

Clause 1
The Devotees

An inspiring Politician[01] is awakened by a penetrating knock on the door; while stroboscopic radiance brightened the night. The color of red overpowered blue as the lights glimmered in the form of states. Immediately the inspiring Politician begins to realize his mission on earth. As the Politician opens the door He is apprehended by two soldiers of the Abeyance.

"For what am I being charged?" He asks.

Refusing to offer any information for captivity, the soldiers simultaneously replied, "Come with us sir." Upon leaving a new Christian Broadcasting Network episode aired featuring numerous citizens that acquired an identical dream of a man riding a white horse from the atmosphere.

While traveling through the Macon county streets of Georgia both soldiers begin to interrogate the Politician. "What's your name sir?" one soldier asks, as the other drives following with the next question, "Where are you from?"

The Politician slowly looks up and stares into the rearview mirror of the armored car, "I am the great I am; King of the Heavens and Earth, Yeshua," answering with a Loud Thundering Accent. Suddenly the car swerves and the eyes of both soldiers turned from white to pinkish red as they began to weep.

From a clear sky, the full moon above revealed a large halo instantly facing the front of the vehicle. While driving towards the moon, the car gradually comes to a stop. The cop on the passenger side opens Yeshua's door and begins to bow; walking over timidly, the driver also bows.

After two minutes elapse the soldiers continue to bow at Yeshua's feet. "Johnny, Pat! We must stay on schedule," Yeshua

01. [pol-i-tish-uhn] a person or king who is bostowed with a sovereign office.

states with a Many Oceans Dialect, overhearing the radio call for both soldiers. Knees shaking, Johnny and Pat slowly stand and begin to wipe their eyes. After making certain Yeshua was in the car comfortably, both soldiers entered as well and continued to the Georgia FEMA camp.

When escorting Yeshua through the entrance to be processed, Johnny and Pat warn Him of the dangers ahead and vow to stay by His side; in response Yeshua replies, "I am covered by my Seraphim. Read my word and spread the news to your loved ones; for I will not be amongst you long." Both Johnny and Pat stared at Yeshua with a facial expression of concern; nevertheless the soldiers began to bow farewell, however Yeshua provided a slight gesture to stop the soldiers' genuflection in full—to avoid a reverence that would invite any attention.

As Yeshua entered the prison, soldiers of the Abeyance aggressively moved Him along. Humbly following the current laws of the land, Yeshua moved with no resistance, but replaced resistance with a smooth perambulate. One soldier noticed the coolness in His walk and took offense, but one look into Yeshua's eyes instantly brought about cowardice. Soldiers of the Abeyance were hardcore mischievous spirited individuals with unbelievable physical strength. Therefore the soldier had to conceal the unexplainable fear, due to embarrassment and possible termination.

Citizens of all ethnic groups and social classes were brutally assaulted as they moved through the "assembly line" to be processed. If any singleton resisted the assault they were shot on the spot by snappers on the balcony above. Observing the madness Yeshua begins to weep, concurrently praying not to anger. Continuing down the line with beatings performed from left to right, Yeshua noticed the line coming to an end. At the end of the line, the solder, there, asked a question that required a yes or no answer: "Do you believe in Jesus?" Yeshua noticed the prison was divided into two sections. All persons who believed in Christ were marked with an X on the left hand and placed on the left section of the prison. All atheist and persons of any other religion were marked with a Y on the left hand and placed in the right.

When Yeshua arrived at the end of the line the soldier asked Him, "Do you believe in Jesus?"

Looking into the soldiers eyes Yeshua replied, "Mark me with a Y."

The soldier did not like the response but fear entered his heart after eye contact; hence without a second thought the soldier marked Yeshua with a Y. Hiding in a nearby room, Johnny and Pat were shocked by Yeshua's answer. Suddenly, they began to realize why He selected to rub shoulders with the non-believers, and rushed to their families to spread the good news.

After all prisoners were processed for the night Yeshua began to pray in a room filled with nonbelievers. Straightaway all eyes were on Him because it was strange to observe a nonbeliever praying to Jehovah. As gunshots were heard from the left section of the prison, a Muslim walked up to Yeshua with a curious look and asked, "Are you Jesus?"

Yeshua looked into his eyes and replied, "Why do you ask about the truth when claim to be a skeptic? Yet why ask a question when you know the truth. You know who I am like I know you Jermaine."

Yeshua looks over the crowd, opens His arms and continues, "Your grandmothers' prayers for you to find Christ were not in vain. Now it is your choice to inherit the kingdom or live in everlasting flame." After asking Christ into their hearts, ten out of thirty atheists including Jermaine—as an act of faith— begged the soldiers to allow them to accompany the children of God; accepting their offer, the Born Again entered the left section of the camp, and shots fired once again.

The remaining atheists engaged in "intellectual conversations" about their successes. As a requirement to leave the camp the "intellects" received the RFID chip in the left hand for surveillance, and were sworn to secrecy; any mention of their whereabouts would result to death. Yeshua was the last prisoner ordered to receive the RFID chip. Before He could refuse, Belial ordered for His immediate release.

Afterwards, Yeshua was flown to an airport in Washington DC and picked up in a secret helicopter headed straight to the White House. When the helicopter arrived on the White House lawn, Yeshua was escorted by two soldiers; as they all disembarked the aircraft. When Yeshua arrived in the Oval Office, Belial patiently stalling, did not waste any time explaining his interest. Sitting at a Parnian radius desk in a recliner with two Generals by his side, Belial states, "Hearkening soldiers of the Abeyance it was brought to my awareness your ability of intimidation, in result I present a proposition." With a body language of arrogance, Belial takes a drink of coffee, and slightly points the cup at Yeshua before placing it on the table, "I motion the opportunity of employment," Belial states with a Lions Accent.

Yeshua looked into Belial's eyes and replied, "You are the ruler of this land and no human is above thee. So as I appear human that would equal thy serving thee. That is blasphemy! For I serve only one and you are not He."

Belial, with a smirk, concurrently showing discomfort straightens his tie and states, "I venerate your current allegiance, and beholding your optics I grasp my soldiers disorganize. I contain jurisdiction over my organization and could not visualize you operating beneath me; whereas you are clearly a frontrunner." Reclining his chair crossing his legs on the table Belial resumes, "There is no uncertainty that I will be elected to a second term, but the election must resemble a race. Have you ever thought of running for office?"

Recollecting the police lights forming states, Yeshua says,

"Although I do not wish to entertain your propositions, prophecy must be fulfilled. For I am the Son given, and evil must end through the Prince of Peace."

With laughter, Belial and the Abeyance attempt to make a mockery out of Yeshua's choice of words, unaware of His moniker, "Excuse my arrogance, I have been in a full conversation and did not unsettle to inquire your name," says Belial, ending with a slight giggle.

"I tell you the truth, you do not realize your arrogance if you do not know me," Yeshua responds and continues, "I will accept the request of the Father and run for the red states." Yeshua humbly asking, "May I be released?" Belial nods his head downwards responding yes, and Yeshua was ushered by two soldiers of the Abeyance.

Secretly Belial ordered the soldiers conveying Yeshua to provide a Visa Black Card, one of the presidential bank accounts valuing twenty million dollars, a Rolls-Royce Phantom, and a house resembling a chateau to inhabit. After the soldiers supplied the riches requested they became confused and somewhat jealous of the treatment; ergo, Yeshua discerned covet in their hearts. "And my God shall supply all your needs according to His riches in glory by Christ Jesus," Yeshua quotes as the soldiers walk towards the castle portal. "The love of money and Satan are one. These riches belong to the Father but are magnified in heaven by: true freedom, natural love, no pain, and no worry. Earthly possessions vanish but heaven is forever."

Yeshua continues as the soldiers alter giving Him their undivided attention, "Set your mind on all things above not on earthly things and you will not be disappointed after death. Many burn eternally and beg for God's mercy when it is too late." Both soldiers walk towards Yeshua after looking into His eyes; when in His presence one bows while the other stands in disbelief. "Shawn and Tim, Belial is expecting you both to serve me, but I am a gentleman and allow free will." Tim begins to bow and Yeshua finishes, "By your actions I receive your answer. Now be free, and do not speak a word of this location; for I am covered by my Seraphim. Read my word and spread the news to your loved ones."

After Shawn and Tim departed, Yeshua called a cab from the castles living area. While waiting, Yeshua began to pray until the cab arrived. Upon entrance, the cab driver slowly drove on the stone driveway, assuming that he arrived at the wrong location. Just to verify the location the cab driver rings the bell. Yeshua's prayer ended as He hears the portals bell. Once the door opened the driver's eyes opened wide slightly stuttering, "Di-did someone call a cab sir?"

Yeshua replied, "Yes," walking towards the back seat as the portal closed behind Him.

When inside the cap, the driver asked, "Where to today sir?" Listening to the radio as the weekly after party was announced.

Yeshua replied, "Let us go to the after party just promoted."

With a surprised facial expression the driver replies, "Are you sure you want to go there?" Subsequently turning up the radio; suddenly showing no interest in an answer to his question. Yeshua looked into the rearview mirror to observe the driver's reaction to the songs played:

Why don't you strip for me baby?
G— d— you bad.
Why don't you strip for me baby?
I wish it was you that I had.
I got a wife, but I wish it was you that I had.
You got a husband, but I wish it was you that I had.

Continuing to the destination the second song played with a screwed voice:

I make it raaain. Call me your Idol, Idol. Call me your Idol.
I make it raaain. Call me your Idol, Idol. Call me your Idol.
It's Saturday: party hard, par, par, par, par, party hard.
It's Saturday: party hard, par, par, par, par, party hard.

Yeshua spent the time praying as the songs prolonged, shortly arriving to the destination another song played through rotation:

I don't care what your parent's saaaay,
I'm-gon-steal-you-from—yo-husband.
We can merk, merk, merk your hubby saaaay,
You-gon-steal-me-from-my-huuusband.
Who we blame it ooon.
Blame-it-on-my-neighbor. Blame-it-on-my-neighbor.
Who we blame it ooon.
Blame-it-on-my-neighbor. Blame-it-on-my-neighbor.

As Yeshua arrived at His destination He was shocked to hear the gobbledygook played on the family radio station. When the driver stopped to ask for cab fare, Yeshua looked into the driver's eyes, and with a Slight Thundering but Many Oceans Dialect He states, "Demarco you should be ashamed to play that station while driving any customer. You wear a cross on your chain but enchant my ears to songs coaching humanity to break all of my Fathers commandments?" Demarco's eyes teemed with tears as he apologized repeatedly for the unknown disrespect. After Demarco asked for forgiveness, he told Yeshua to keep the Taxi fare for the tithes he failed to subsidize over the years. "Now that your eyes are open to the message in that music there is no excuse. Read my word and spread the news to your loved ones; for I will not be amongst you long," Yeshua states as He exits the cab.

Walking towards the club around Eleven O'clock Post Meridiem, Yeshua witnesses an enormous line headed towards a building playing music similar to the radio station in the Taxi. While Yeshua waited in the line for about twenty minutes, clubbers communicated with profanities from left to right in relation to Yeshua, unaware of His presence: some claiming how they would make it rain in VIP, while others had additional meaningless conversations. Yeshua stood in the line for thirty minutes until he was stopped by a bouncer, asking for an ID at the entrance. After exhibiting the Visa Black Card, Yeshua was allowed to enter without an Identification Card. One of the thugs in the line witnessed Yeshua present the Visa Black Card and thievery immediately entered his mind.

When Yeshua continued through the club His heart saddened, witnessing women made in His Fathers image remove their cloths for money. Suddenly the DJ introduces a dancer to the stage, "Now, for the moment you have all been waiting for. Coming to the stage.... Passion! All yall broke pimps move to the back. This is the real show."

After Yeshua saw Passion, He instantly recognized her heart and knew she was a diehard worshiper. Recognizing she was the focal point of His visitation, Yeshua departed the club; upon departure the thug who watched Yeshua pull out His Visa Black Card rounded his crew, and four thugs followed Yeshua out of the club.

While Yeshua waited on Passion outside of the club He felt a presence, and as He turned around the thug pulled out a gun, "Let me get that. If you resist it won't be a good look for you dread cat," the thug stated, threatening Yeshua to give up His wallet.

Yeshua looked into His eyes and stated, "Akili I do not know you, but I know your mother, who prays every day for you to change your ways. The meaning of your name is smart and bright, but even the demons who possess you do not step to me.

My word states to give to those who ask, but I must deny you of my Visa Card for your own protection. Look at your associates, for they are held by my Seraphim and my Seraphim are trained for battle beyond your imagination, but to honor my word I will give my shirt, and as a coat I will spare your life." After the Seraphim released the thugs, scared for his life, Akili took Yeshua's shirt and made scarce with his associates.

Witnessing the robbery, an atheist from the FEMA camp recognized Yeshua and proceeded to provide assistance, as he removed his shirt—that by coincidence matched Yeshua's pants—the man uttered, "Take my shirt sir," and walked away with no remorse for rejecting Jesus a second time. An hour passed as Yeshua saw Passion leaving the club walking His way.

Pacing behind Passion followed one of the bouncers, as both walked by Yeshua the bouncer grabbed Passion attempting to pull her in his car. Passion screaming for help, Yeshua grappled the bouncer towards Him and looked into His eyes, "Let her go Bobo," Yeshua stated with a Thundering Accent.

Bobo held up his hands amazed and frightened as he realized who was confronting him, and walked away ashamed as Passion ran to her vehicle. Yeshua then sits at a bus stop while Passion gathers herself, and afterwards, she slowly rolls upon Him. "Do you need a ride?" She asked with a Puerto Rican Accent.

Yeshua smiles replying, "Yes I do," enters the car and Passion departed the scene.

While driving to the palace Passion played "Hallelujah" by Lecrae. Still smiling, Yeshua asked, "What do you know about that?"

"That is my song. What you think? Just because I am a stripper I don't love God? I have to pray every night before I go on that stage with wayward spirits fawning at my body. I'm telling you if my little daughter and son were not born I would not be there, but I have to do what I got to do." Passion continues, glancing quickly at Yeshua and back at the road noticing she is talking to a stranger, "I don't even know why I picked you up. You could be one of those creeps at the club, but something told me to pick you up. I don't know what it is."

Shortly approaching Yeshua's palace, Passion states, "I have never been in this area before. What are you rich? That may be the reason I felt I should pick you up. I always run across successful wealthy men but they always end up creeps. It seems like I have a bad judge of character. I'm sick of the same cycle over and over. I pray I come across a great man one day."

Before pulling into the stone driveway Yeshua gently instructed Passion to stop, preventing her from viewing the castle, and looked into Passion's eyes. "I do not ever remember you complaining Kirtana. You usually spend most of your time praying. I guess the saying is true. He may not be there when you want Him, but The Lord always comes on time," Yeshua states with His Many Oceans Dialect.

Suddenly Kirtana Miguel cries simultaneously hugging Yeshua relentlessly. "I knew you were coming," Kirtana weeps with rapture. Yeshua then instructs Kirtana to pull into the stone driveway and stop at the portal.

"Now look up, this is your kingdom on earth. You and your children will not want or need any longer. Do you see that luxury vehicle? It is yours with no payments. I only ask of you one favor," Yeshua says. "Be my vice president; for I am running against Belial to take revenge against the persecution of God's children."

Kirtana, addled on why Yeshua picked her replied, "But why me Lord. I am just a stripper at the Camlot. Who will respect me knowing my last profession?"

"I know your heart, and I know your potential," Yeshua replies. "Any stone thrower will soon meet their judgment. And this world is full of sin."

Accepting Yeshua's request Kirtana asked about the campaign strategy. Yeshua states, "The approach is simple. Provide true change. First we minister to the street and provide the homeless shelter. Second we provide the jobless employment by creating jobs. And in return we will save lost souls by revealing the truth in a world full of lies." Yeshua explains further, "I will provide talents you never knew you could possess. We will change the schools. We will change the church. We will change government. We will change music. We will change television. We will change commerce. We will teach love. Saints will own businesses, and Saints will own banks. Saints will enforce the law. Saints will be the lawyers and the judges, ruling to please the highest Judge of all."

Upon entering the castle Kirtana could not believe her eyes. She begin to witness how prayers of faith accumulate dreams into reality. Suddenly she dropped to her knees and interceded outwardly as Yeshua prayed silently. The prayer secession resembled marital love as both came into agreement with The Father. After an hour of praying, Yeshua and Kirtana planned their strategy to acquire office and establish righteousness within Columbia and the world.

Yeshua explained how the both of them would espouse twelve respected individuals in the states holding the highest amount of electoral votes, and those individuals will be called the Devotees: "We will have two Devotees in each state: California, Texas, Florida, Illinois, New York, and Philadelphia. All Devotees will have a background in charity or desire to have a reputation of benevolence," Yeshua stated, setting the destinations for their immaculate journey. Yeshua and Kirtana hired a company called Fashion Squad (FS) to assist with their attire, as they prepared for the task ahead. Ready for the battle against Belial, Yeshua and Kirtana entered the Rolls-Royce headed to New York, in expedition of the first two Devotees.

Before entering New York, Yeshua and Kirtana stopped at a convenience store for gas. Since Kirtana was well known from Washington to New York for her past profession, she saw a group of men who recognized her. The heathens ungraciously provide an ovation, "Pas-sion, Pas-sion, Pas-sion" in a chant as Kirtana walks into the store. After paying for the gas Kirtana walked back to the car as one of the heathens yell, "Who is that in the car your new sugar daddy?" The group laughs as Yeshua exits the passenger seat.

Walking up to the heathens, Yeshua looks into their eyes one by one and states, "Galvin, Nero, Jalil, and Raheem how can you all judge when your street pharmacy pollutes humanity? Kirtana is my future vice president, and she will assist in saving the humanity you help destroy. Before you throw stones take the advice of your mothers and grandmothers who pray for you to change your ways." The drug dealers were amazed but walked away ashamed as they realized who confronted them, while Yeshua and Kirtana continued to New York City.

After arriving in New York City, Yeshua and Kirtana continued to Manhattan. While advancing they came upon a man who appeared destitute holding a sign stating, "The end is coming soon. Repent for your sins." Yeshua instructed Kirtana to stop, and she then witnessed how although vagrant, the man received the attention of a superstar. "Do you see that man?" Yeshua says. "That is our first Devotee." Without questioning Yeshua, ensuing Kirtana's parking of the vehicle, she walks up to and converses with the homeless man.

"Would you like a ride?" Kirtana asks jovially.

"Why would you like to offer a man like myself a ride in a vehicle like yours?" the homeless man replied with a suave Noo Yawk Accent, flabbergasted by the interest in him.

"Well first I do not judge books by their covers; but since you asked, I feel your story is more interesting than any wealthy individual walking through Manhattan," Kirtana says.

"How can you determine this by my appearance?" replied the man.

"I am a good judge of character thus says The Lord. Now come, so I can get you out of those cloths," ended Kirtana, as they both departed the thoroughfare.

Kirtana and the homeless man enter the car as the man notices Yeshua. "So how can I assist you distinguished individuals this evening?" the man states with a curious gawk.

Yeshua looked into his eyes and told his story. "You are a man of great faith, and hear the voice of The Lord ceaselessly. You are homeless only by choice, and for your obedience come great reward. Now Shawn, be one of my Devotees; for I am running against Belial to take revenge against the persecution of God's children."

Shawn Dacso was overly honored and bowed his head holding Yeshua's hand as he realized who offered him employment. "I welcome your offer through the soul that dwells within," Shawn states accepting Yeshua's offer.

"Now let's get a presidential suite to get you out of those cloths," Kirtana says genuinely but with a sense of humor.

When Yeshua, Kirtana, and Shawn arrived at The Four Seasons, all eyes were on Shawn due to his appearance. Kirtana began to get upset, howbeit Yeshua reminded her of the character she must maintain. "How may I help you on this day?" The front desk clerk states sarcastically.

"We have a reservation for President Yeshua," Kirtana replied meekly, trying to stay professional.

"President Yeshua!? I make all the reservations and I unquestionably do not recall a President Yeshua," the overcompensated clerk replies with vainglory.

Looking into the clerks eyes Yeshua states, "Look again." Glazing into Yeshua's eyes the clerk recognized who confronted her and omitted the reservations to provide Kirtana with a key and room number. Apologizing for her snobbishness she offers to resign from clerk to be Yeshua's bellhop. Yeshua states, "I do not wish that you leave your position. Be mindful of the arrogance towards your peers Elizabeth. In return, read and spread my word to anyone who will listen." Elizabeth began to weep as Yeshua, Kirtana, and Shawn continued to the suite.

When Shawn entered the suite with Yeshua and Kirtana he could not believe his eyes. Yeshua went in the next room to pray, and Shawn began to tell Kirtana his story in its entirety; ensuing her call to the New York Fashion Squad. "I was once a wealthy man well respected in my community. I was an attorney employed by Wilton Bates, a famous law firm in Manhattan. My face stayed in the news for my charity cases as I netted my fortune through endorsements. Then one day, Wilton Bates ordered me to take the case for a senator now known as President Belial. They claimed that I could become rich from the ... case." Shawn explains, pausing as he begins to feel uneasy, not knowing whether to continue on the topic of Belial.

"What was the case about?" Kirtana replied confused in regards to the pause in his speech.

Before Shawn could say another word Yeshua interrupted, "Shawn, do not continue. We must be cautious of our surroundings."

Suddenly the phone rings, slightly startled but unafraid, Kirtana and Shawn look at one another with wonderment. After answering the phone Kirtana learned about the Fashion Squad's arrival at the front desk, and she accepted their company as Shawn went to take a lavation. After he freshened up, the Fashion Squad persisted to make Shawn far and above presentable. When walking to the front desk Elizabeth nearly drooled in Shawn's presence, further embarrassed on how she previously portrayed herself; while Yeshua, Kirtana, and Shawn left the luxury hotel into the Rolls-Royce to find the second Devotee.

Throughout the midnight expedition about the Brooklyn

streets, all eyes were on the Rolls-Royce. Continuing down the cold streets they noticed three prostitutes. Yeshua instructed Kirtana to stop, and He exited the passenger seat. As Yeshua approached the women a pimp walked behind Him from a distance. "Let me talk to you over here yo. I can help with the prices," the pimp savagely yelled.

Ignoring the pimp, Yeshua proceeded to approach the street walkers. Alternating His head, Yeshua looks into the eyes of two prostitutes and states, "Olympia and Shanese you two were well respected women in Philadelphia. Why do you let a man control your Godly thoughts? Turn away from your sins, and I will provide your kingdom on earth."

Shawn saw the pimp scuttle towards Yeshua and tackled him to the ground. Siblings Olympia and Shanese Olive bow at Yeshua's feet. "Hallelujah, hallelujah," Shanese utters repeatedly in soulful Mid-Atlantic Dialect; while Olympia whispers, "Thank You Jesus, thank You Jesus," repeatedly in a Patois of Vendée yet Mid-Atlantic Dialect; both accepting to turn away from their fornication. The third prostitute considered the use of profanities against Yeshua to express her disapproval, but when He looked into her eyes she could not speak half of a blasphemy, as He scared her demons.

"Every knee will bow, in heaven and on earth and under the earth, and every tongue will confess that Jesus Christ is Lord," Yeshua states, as the pimp and the third prostitute bowed. Suddenly able to control themselves, the pimp and the third prostitute ran off collectively; while Yeshua, Shawn, Olympia, and Shanese entered the Rolls-Royce.

Olympia and Shanese were noticeably appreciative as they realized their nightmare instantly altered into a dream. When driving towards the suite Kirtana changed the radio to a famous station called "Christian talk." The station was founded to provide guidance for women just leaving the club. A well-known Disc Jockey named Foxy Fox spoke about how to convince men to postpone intercourse until marriage. Kirtana, Olympia, and Shanese began to rave about the topic and the radio show, confirming that the show was eminent among women across Columbia. Shanese continued to explain how Foxy Fox was an old friend of hers who lived in Brookville, New York. Yeshua, predestining the next Devotee, directed Kirtana to the radio station in which Foxy Fox broadcasted.

After arriving at the station Shanese guided Kirtana to Foxy Fox's vehicle. While waiting for Foxy, Olympia noticed a man with a dozen roses slowly pacing back and forth at the stations entrance. After wandering about, the stranger finally positioned against a wall neighboring the doorway. Eventually around Five Thirty Ante Meridiem, the morning DJ, Ricky Jones, walked towards the door acknowledging the man as they engaged in small talk. Following two minutes of polite conversation Ricky entered the station. About ten minutes later Foxy Fox departures the front door, and after observing the flower man she distinctly denied any conversation.

Yeshua exits the Rolls-Royce as Foxy and the flower man squabble at the entrance; after walking up to Foxy, He states, "Rachelle, for the anger of man does not produce the righteousness of God." Now looking into Foxy Fox's eyes, Yeshua continues, "Be angry and do not sin; do not let the sun go down on your anger, and give no opportunity to the devil."

Chronically staring in Yeshua's eyes..., "I looked up the same bible verses about anger the other day," Rachelle "Foxy Fox" Casydi states in a Patois Accent. Recognizing who confronted her, she begins to cry bowing at Yeshua's feet.

"Who are you calling the devil? Only God can judge me." The flower man says with a Southern Twang, directing his statement towards Yeshua. "And who are you to think you can cut in the middle of my conversation like I am not here? And why are you bowing to him Foxy?" The flower man quotes a verse from the bible, "See that you are not led astray. For many will come in my name, saying, 'I am he!' and, 'The time is at hand!' Do not go after them."

Yeshua looks into the flower man's eyes and states, "Pastor Booker, you study my words but still do not know me. As you look into my eyes you still wonder if your eyes deceive you. Many of your church members left and are now lost souls. I tell you the truth, their blood is on your hands."

Pastor Booker, eyes-wide-exposed,†[02] drops to his knees with his head bowed and states, "Sorry I did not recognize you Lord, I am chagrined in the way that I addressed you, and equally embarrassed about the words I did not speak and were revealed."

Yeshua pulls up Pastor Booker's head and states, "Find any member who left your church and humbly give your testimony about my second coming. They will believe, knowing that you are not an easily swayed man. Convince them to rededicate themselves to Christ and save your own soul." Yeshua invites his right hand to Pastor Booker, pulling him ascendant to settle on his feet. After standing, Pastor Booker urgently sauntered on his enterprise to unearth the members that departed his sanctuary.

Yeshua walked Rachelle to her vehicle where Shanese and Olympia waited patiently. Shanese, Olympia, and Rachelle surrounded the car as Yeshua humbly conciliated the sinners to join the Devotees. After cheerfully accepting Yeshua's overture, everyone entered their vehicles, and Rachelle shadowed the Rolls Royce to the Four Seasons presidential suite.

After arriving at the suite a team of internet news reporters awaited Yeshua due to rumors of a possible Jesus return. Rachelle pulled up beside the Rolls-Royce with the driver's window down and Kirtana stated, "What do you want to do my Deity? We can flee the scene and find another hotel if it is too early to reveal your return."

02. spiritual eyes open; in tune with the Spirit of Truth

"No," Yeshua answers, "Most will not believe because they have not all seen the heavens open with The One called Faithful and True riding a white horse, but it was so as I came like a thief in the night. Word of my presence have extended far behold any news reporter; for many are still in search of hells gate. I will not deny any individual in search of the truth."

Rachelle preserved every word on her mobile voice recorder as she held it out of the window. Kirtana pulled up to the reporters as the current Devotees exited both vehicles; Yeshua exiting the Rolls-Royce.

One reporter inquires, "There are rumors Jesus returned to save the earth as we know it. Are you him?"

Following another with an inquisition, "And I heard you were running for president, is that true?"

The third reporter catechizes, "I heard you were seen in a strip club, and mingling with some prostitutes from Philadelphia. Is that true?"

Following the fourth with a catechization, "If you are Christ why do you ride in a Rolls-Royce? Doesn't the word say money is the root of all evil?"

In response to the reporters as a whole Yeshua states, "For my thoughts are not your thoughts, neither are your ways my ways. For as the heavens are higher than the earth, so are my ways higher than your ways, and my thoughts than your thoughts." All reporters were left with their mouths wide open and their vision restored from blindness; as Yeshua walked into the Four Seasons with Kirtana and the current Devotees following.

Making it a point to correct the word..., "And it's the love of money is the root of all evil," Rachelle states with a trivial He-told-you-attitude.

After walking back into the Four Seasons, Elizabeth greeted Yeshua and The Devotees like celebrities specifically trying to get Shawn's attention. Before entering the elevator Elizabeth's manager approached Yeshua. "Elizabeth has been an extraordinary employee following you all's first confrontation. May I ask the nature of your conversation?" the manager femininely asked.

"When pride comes, then comes disgrace, but with humility comes wisdom," Yeshua replied looking into the manager's eyes, "Pete, do not allow the media to excuse your sins. Repent! And save your own soul!" Pete begins to weep knowing who confronted him and walked away with no yearning to prolong his past life style.

As soon as Shanese, Olympia, and Rachelle entered the suite they exceedingly grasped the benefits of living for God; as facial expressions of amazement revealed their cogitation.

Yeshua walked into the master bedroom to pray while Kirtana untangled the responsibilities of the current Devotees. "You are the first four Devotees and eight more are required to complete our sovereignty. The remaining Devotees will be elected by our Deity, and such were all of you. Although I was appointed to Vice President, I am not worthy and further became conscious of The Almighty's grace." Kirtana continues, tearing up, "Shawn you will be the Lawyer who will reconstruct one bisect of Columbia's court system. The other half will be a judge not yet selected." Excusing her tears Kirtana continues, "Rachelle, you will transform shortwave as one of the top DJ personalities ever. Olympia and Shanese, you two will change street life throughout Columbia and world, encouraging women to abandon the thoroughfare and follow Christ. In all, every Devotee will collectively embolden more sinners to become their celestial selves."

As Kirtana spoke she noticed the extremity for a spacious vehicle, and made an appointment in Hollywood California to procure an Elemment Palazzo; following another call to order one million sacred writings. On the call succeeding Kirtana ordered Olympia and Shanese first class tickets to California; and the remaining Devotees, Yeshua, and herself economy class.

The assemblage schmoozed while patiently waiting for Yeshua's return. After praying for an hour and a half to The Father, Yeshua walked back into the living area with celestial brilliance.

When arriving at the airport Kirtana divided the airline tickets respectively. Yeshua, observing how Kirtana ordered the tickets, smiled pulling Kirtana to the side. "I am proud of you and your logic in ordering the tickets," Yeshua states. "Our presence is much needed in coach. As well as Olympia and Shanese presence in first class. It is time for God's children to reap the benefits for their sacrifices in Christ for the world to witness, in result removing one of Satan's greatest tactics. The purpose of my word is not to yearn for poverty. There is no truth in the Devil. My purpose is for you to live prosperous but not worship earthly treasures."

The Devotees, Yeshua, and Kirtana enter the plane, and as hours pass arrive at Los Angeles International Airport. Kirtana made arrangements for the Elemment Palazzo to be parked in front of the LAX's Encounter Restaurant while the crew banqueted. After nourishment, Kirtana surprised the Devotees with her choice of transportation. The Devotees conducted as teenyboppers after setting eyes on the luxury mobile home, and Yeshua was pleased after noticing the innocence of their enjoyment.

Maneuvering in downtown Los Angeles, Kirtana waited on Yeshua to elect the next Devotee. Approaching the Staples Center, Yeshua instructed Kirtana to park in a lot near the entrance. Yeshua and Shawn exited the vehicle; Shawn wafted the sacred writings, graciously refusing to allow Yeshua to perform any manual moonlight. As they headed to the Stadium a large crowd waited at the ticket gate. A banner below the Staples Center's sign indicated Faye O—a famous pop singer—would be performing live at Nine Post Meridiem.

Yeshua advanced towards the Guest Services Center to inquire about VIP tickets. Rudely, the employee at the front desk replied, "Groupies, groupies, groupies. Faye O does not accept VIP at her shows. So, Fo sheedo find another hutch to stalk mark, ooohhhh." The employee screams holding his heart.

Yeshua reached over and touched the man's chest looking into his eyes. "The Lord is merciful and gracious, slow to anger, and abounding in mercy," Yeshua states as the man's health is restored. "For whoever curses his father or his mother shall be put to death." Yeshua removing His hand from Chico's chest continues, "Chico, your tattoo states 'Jesus is Lord', and Lord is The Father. So it is only mercy that keeps you breathing."

Chico pleads for mercy as he temporarily leaves his job to bow at Yeshua's feet. A crowd of people witnessed the healing and stared in amazement. A man who happened to be Faye O's manager, Taye Boii, overheard Yeshua ask for a VIP ticket, and after witnessing the healing felt obligated to take Yeshua back stage while Faye O performed. "I don't know what it is about you sir, and knowing O, I may be bounced for doing this but follow me," stated Taye Boii. The silly crowd was further amazed when observing Yeshua with Taye Boii, now pondering His identity.

Millions of fans watched Faye O perform her new hot single "Jesus Think I'm sexy," while singing the chorus, the crowd yells in a Nan, Na, Na, Nan Na, You Can't Catch Me Rhythm and paralleling Witch Voice, "Jesus think I'm seXy but I'm-not, im-pressed, I like to, party-like-the-rest, in love with, arch-fiend-breast." Suddenly while singing Faye O shakes—as if experiencing a seizure—and collapses on stage.

Adherents in multitudes squawked in reaction to Faye O's episode. Yeshua emerged on stage looked into Faye O's eyes and thundered, "Mikey, Damon, and Vicky!"

Faye O, still shaking and unconscious, Mikey replied in a baby voice, "It is not time. Why are you here?"

Damon the writer stated, "Leave us be she wants to be with us now."

Vicky with a witch voice stated, "Please don't, please don't, please leave, don't maul me!"

Yeshua replied to the three spirits collectively, "Be quite all of you, and come out of her!" Suddenly Faye O's convulsing ceased, and Yeshua carried her off of the stage, absent from the spotlight.

The speechless crowd walked towards the exit: some asking for a reimbursement, while others were apprehensive about Faye O's health. As immense concourse exited the stadium, the Devotees handed out bibles, and in unison spoke to the rabble about what they just witnessed.

"I was lost on the street and Jesus rescued my sister and me from prostitution, letting us know that we did not need to befriend Satan to gain wealth," Shanese told the crowd catching their attention by her picturesque appearance. Olympia conversed with another group while she attracted a different crowd due to her opposite yet chocolate-box appearance.

An internet news crew accompanied the crowd while the Devotees enunciated and handed out testaments. The reporters buttonholed the crowd as they left the Devotees to schlepp towards their car. From the departing crowd, most facial expressions were mien of confusion and worry, pondering Armageddon, while others walked away with an urgency to read the bible in order to get their lives together. Many atheists protested the concert to the reporters labeling it unconstitutional.

Four additional teams of internet reporters approached the scene as Kirtana reported her testimony to the crowd, "I was once one of the top paid exotic dancers in District of Columbia, making over one thousand dollars a day; but Jesus delivered me from that situation and I will be His running mate as He battles Belial for President." Kirtana continues, and as her crowd grew, she handed out testaments, "Now read this book and make your prediction on who wins the red states, also known as Jesusland."

"I was a lawyer ..." Shawn begun, laughing as he notices people beginning to depart, "Wait, wait, wait don't leave I am one of the just lawyers. I refused to take a case that would have made me one of the wealthiest men in America, simply because it did not settle correctly within my gut. I am here to tell you, now I ride in an Elemment Palazzo; Jesus is not boring like the serpent would have most think. He wants you just how you are, and He wants us to be kings and queens."

Rachelle received attention from the largest crowd, whereas a majority of the concourse noticed her voice from her famous after the club radio show. "Foxy Fox on the ones and twos representing who-who. You know me and who I represent G-O-D all day Boo-Boo. By the way I want to give a Special shout out to President Yeshua. He will be handing down Special beatings to Belial come this November. A real change is coming soon my people very soon."

Backstage Yeshua continued to rehabilitate Faye O while Taye Boii and her dancers eagle-eyed with concern. About two minutes passed and Faye O regained consciousness. Yeshua looked into Faye O's eyes and stated, "Janeth Grace, you have not been yourself since your Papa died. I am here to tell you, John-John wants you to continue living."

Knowing that no one knew her Grandpa's name, "Like, who are you? And how do you know my Grandpa's government?" Faye O stated in a Valley Girl Accent, confused as to whom confronted her.

Yeshua states, "You have been possessed with sprints of the earth's core. So it is no surprise you do not recognize me from looking into my optic. Take this doctrine; the first page in which you turn will explain who I am and how I know your Grandpa's name. The second will explain how you can see him again." Yeshua slightly looked into Taye Boii's eyes turned and walked away from Faye O's entourage.

After departing Faye O, Yeshua headed to the front of the Staples Center, where the Devotee's crowd was nearly cleared. Half of the bibles were handed out and more than half of the crowd gave their lives to Christ.

The remaining crowd waited to view Yeshua up close and personal. Yeshua knowing the starvation of the remaining crowd stated, "I suppose you would have never believed until you witnessed signs and wonders! I know all your health request and I say to the blind man see. I say to the woman with an injured womb, bear a female child and name her Manna. I say to every cancer patient, the believers who wore pink attire on your behalf was not in vain; be healed. I say to every adulterer, I have healed your gouged eyes, see your Virtuous woman. Every non-believer accompanied by a healed believer, your souls are now healed; for you have witnessed signs and wonders."

Still backstage Faye O comforted her manager, "Who let that man backstage?" Every hanger-on looked at one another with an "It-wasn't-me" rubberneck. Instantly the room flooded with finger-pointing grapevine. Tired of the chaos, "I let him backstage," Taye Boii confesses aggressively to clear the air. All and sundry stared at Taye Boii outlandishly except Faye O, giving an intriguing facial expression.

Faye O pulled Taye Boii aside, and before Faye O could say a word.... "That man is not just any man. He delivered you from a state that I have never seen in any person. I have been in church where people were relieved from evil spirits, but this was different," Taye Boii said nervously.

"Who do you think he was?" asked Faye O, continuing her intriguing stare.

"III'm afraid to sssay," Taye Boii slightly stuttered. "We have been making a lot of money with our secular grooves ... just open the bible he gave you and whatever you decide to do

I'm down."

Picking up the bible, Faye O inadvertently turned to Jeremiah One:Nine, "Before I formed you in the womb I knew you, and before you were born I consecrated you; I appointed you a prophet to the nations," Faye O read to herself with confusion, knowing she has not cared for God since her grandpa died. "This message could not have been for me," Faye O states to Taye Boii.

"You know I know you inside and out O. I remember when we were younger; you used to talk about God continuously. And after your granddaddy passed away you did a one eighty and completely denied Him," Taye Boii states.

"You are tripping," Faye O quickly responds

"For real O, you know I'm going to keep it real," Taye Boii replies immediately.

"What does God have to do with the man that just left?" Faye O states.

"Go find Him and ask Him," Taye Boii suggested. Faye O ran outside—Taye Boii convoying—to catch up with the man who saved her life.

After finishing with the crowd, about twenty minutes passed as Yeshua and the Devotees waited for Faye O in the Elemment Palazzo. "My Deity, I don't think Faye O is coming." Kirtana stated concerned about Yeshua's emotional state.

"God opposes the proud, but gives grace to the humble," Yeshua responds. "Be patient she is coming." Soon to follow a fretted Faye O hurried about desperately searching for the man who saved her. Spotting the Elemment Palazzo, Faye O approached the mobile home in high hopes that the driver had information about the mystery man.

When Faye O verged upon the vehicle she perceived Yeshua standing with all of His Excellency. Yeshua looked into Faye O's eyes, Faye O still blind from the evil sprints that once possessed her was still not aware of Yeshua's denomination. "So, I opened the bible you gave me and read the verse. Look ... if you can tell me...."

Yeshua graciously interrupting Faye O states, "Before I formed you in the womb I knew you Mi Mi, and before you were born I consecrated you; I appointed you a prophet to the nations." Faye O stood with her mouth wide open as Yeshua continued.

... "That is the verse you silently quoted in the bible," Yeshua stated, completing Faye O's sentence beforehand. "Now turn back to Jeremiah One:Nine, the verse you turn to in the bible."

Faye O opened the closed book with no crinkles on the pages from the last browsing. Yeshua extended His pointer and middle finger, touching Faye O's mouth as she silently read, "Look, I have put my words in your mouth. See, I have set you this day over nations and over kingdoms, to pluck up and to break down, to destroy and to overthrow, to build and to plant." Yeshua states while an amazed Faye O perused. "Now turn to the second page as I instructed, and you will find how to see your PaPa after this life."

The second page in which Faye O turned was Jeremiah Five:Twelve, "But instead you and your followers have spoken falsely towards me, producing as they enjoyed compositions that mock me and have said, He will do nothing; no disaster will come upon us, nor shall we see sword or famine. Therefore I say, because you have spoken these words, look, I am making my words in your mouth a fire, and your followers wood, and the fire shall consume them. I am bringing against you O, house of New Secular.†⁰³ Choose for yourself this day whom you will serve, but if you deny me again by refusing to pluck up, break down, destroy and overthrow the grooves that you contributed,

---

03. [noo-sek-yuh-ler] the music generation in which mocks the Lord; music made by the chief one's - rev. Isaiah 14:9-11

John John's dwelling is not yours," Yeshua states, looking into Faye O's eyes.

Dropping to her knees, Faye O bows at Yeshua's feet finally noticing who comforted her. Taye Boii seizing the moment begins to bow as well. "I am totally repentant My Deity. Please forgive me for all my wrongdoings. I will cheerfully oblige, and bring into being the compositions of your desire," Faye O states joining the Devotees. Taye Boii however walked away downhearted, not inclined to change from the machine that made him affluent.

Faye O promenaded to the back while Kirtana and Rachelle's position alternated leaving Rachelle the designated driver. While traveling, Kirtana and Faye O further conversed about Faye O's position and the objectives of the Devotees. Understanding the Devotees desideratum for a movie director, Faye O scrutinized her Stuart Hughes iPhone 4 accessing twitter for any events.

"That is a nice phone girrrl, Big Balling O," Kirtana states laughing.

"Thank you honey and I got it free too. You know Stuart Hughes was my sponsor. They gave it to me on one of my commercials, you knooow, but that was in my BC days,"†[04] Faye O states, ending with a giggle.

"BC days, girl you just got saved a second ago," Kirtana says continuing to laugh.

"I know right," Faye O states continuing to giggle.

Yeshua provided a slight glaze at Faye O, and after their eyes connected, Faye O felt conviction regarding the one million dollar cell phone. "You know, I feel obligated to develop a celebrity eBay account, and I am going to market this phone along with some of my other possessions," Faye O tells Kirtana with

---

04. Before Christ; before one finds and is saved by Christ, towards the road to righteousness.

a gander of concern. Looking out of the window recognizing two displaced individuals with their heads down, Faye O continues, "And I am going to sell my mansion also. With the money I am going to provide vehicles to as many needy families as possible, maybe even open an expensive apartment complex for the displaced."

"Sounds remarkable, let's make that happen," Kirtana tells Faye O, as Yeshua provides a stare and smile of approval, advancing to the master room to pray. Suddenly, Faye O hears a tweet from her phone's Twitter. One of her celebrity followers tweeted about a social gathering involving directors from the movie industry. Kirtana using her golden judgment agreed to Faye O's recommendation, and Faye O directed Rachelle to the next destination.

Upon entering the proximate stop, Yeshua noticed a gentleman with his head down in situ, while the others entered the affair. After instructing Rachelle to stop, Yeshua walked towards the castaway and took a squat neighboring him. "Do you really desire to mingle with the damned? Isn't my love greater than any heathen at this gathering?" Yeshua states as the man looks into His eyes. "I have noticed your compromise for my name sake. Now come with me Joannes, and intermingle with the blessed."

Joannes Casting bowed at Yeshua's feet knowing who confronted him, "Thank you Jesus," he states with an Asian accent. A bevy of groupies cachinnated forthwith, while Joannes showed reverence. Faye O noticed the cluster of femme fatale and their disrespect towards Yeshua. Knowing that her "celebrity status" would influence the women actions, she abandoned the mobile home to bow along with Joannes. When the groupies recognized Faye O they began to shriek scrambling towards her.

"What peace, so long as the whoredoms of thy mother Jezebel and her witchcrafts are so many?" Yeshua states once the groupies were in His presence, afterwards, He looked down at

Faye O with a smile, pleased with the reason that she departed the mobile home to show reverence.

One groupie possessed a displeased facial expression, while the others giggled collectively, after hearkening Yeshua's statement. "Judith isn't your mother's name Jezebel?" one groupie states while the others continue to laugh, concurrently waiting for an autograph from Faye O.

"And how disrespectful to titter while one shows reverence to the Lord," Yeshua states; looking at the groupies with a glare of disappointment.

The groupie with a displeased facial expression stated, "You are no Lord to me and I don't know why Faye O is even bowing to you. Faye O music is cool and she acts a fool on camera, I can respect her for that, but like her song says, bowing to you she is 'confused as shh—'" Before the groupie could even speak half of a blasphemy she caresses her heart in pain, as Yeshua looks into her eyes.

One groupie yelled, "Oh my God."

Another cried, "Call nine-one-one," while the others stood in trepidation.

Faye O and Joannes composedly stood next to Yeshua as the three stare at the groupie collapse from cardiac arrest. The other groupies wondered about in a daze, as if they practiced somnambulism, waiting on the ambulance to arrive.

Suddenly the ambulance arrived, and the medics place the groupie on a stretcher to apply pads on her chest. One medic says, "Clear!" performing defibrillation to regain a heartbeat. Repeating the same procedure after three tries, the medics pull a cover over the groupie indicating that she was deceased.

More individuals gathered while the medics proceeded to the ambulance. After placing the stretcher into the vehicle, out of the blue, a stranger pulls out a gun and aims at the driver of the ambulance. "Get out of the car, you know what this is. Move quickly or it's going to be two deaths instead of one on today."

With two hands up the driver exits the ambulance. Afterwards the thug pulls up to Faye O—as she and Joannes walk towards the Elemment Palazzo—and attempt to force her in the vehicle. "Yea I love that song you did 'If You Had One Night.' And I told myself one day when watching that video. If I ever see her I'm going to force her to give me a night. Now get into the ambulance before the scene turns more ugly," the thug states pointing the gun towards Faye O's head.

Faye O remains calm showing no sign of fear, smiles and says, "You have no idea."

"What bit—" before the thug could speak half of a blasphemy, Yeshua opens the door.

"Jack, before you shot a gun you must have ammunition," Yeshua states as the man turns from Faye O to point the gun at Him. Now looking into the thug's eyes Yeshua continues, "The reason you have breath this second is because of my mercy. Now Jack, leave the gun with me before you are tempted to load it in the future. Read my word and turn towards the light; for I will not be amongst you long."

Hand shaking, Jack dropped the gun and ran out of the ambulance. Subsequent to witnessing Jack run, the groupies and medics sprint towards the back of the ambulance. After reaching the vehicle, one groupie attempts to open the back door.

"Ma'am, please back away from the vehicle we have to go," one medic states.

"No this is my best friend, she is not going anywhere without me," one groupie states while the other groupies pettifog with the medics.

Yeshua walks towards the group in the back of the ambulance and states, "Your friend has been deceased for ten minutes and not one of you has prayed." Progressing to walk up to the deceased woman Yeshua continues, "Victoria your grandmother's prayer for you to live has been answered. Now get up! And listen to your grandmother's spiritual advice; for I will not be amongst you long."

While Yeshua perambulated towards the mobile home, the crowd was awestruck after contemplating Victoria settle to her feet—as if they just encountered an apparition. After realism settled, the medics continued to stand in amazement while the groupies blubbered, inseparably giving Victoria a clasp welcome.

"Where did Jesus go?" Victoria asked her friends after realizing she was among the living. The enchanters laughed as one sarcastically states, "Jesus!? Girl you must have been in heaven when you died, ha-ha-ha."

Victoria's best friend stared at her with a confused but serious stare as Victoria states, "No merry-andrews I wasn't in heaven, I'm talking about the man who brought me back to life, where is He?"

"How did you know he brought you back to life? And why did you call him Jesus?" asked Victoria's best friend.

"I actually did not go to heaven, I was with the devil, and the only light was from the man who revived me. Now you know how we go to these parties to enchant the rich for money, using scopolamine to influence their every action. We have to stop. I have to start listening to my grandmother."

Victoria begins to cry as she finishes, "I was demented the way I spoke to Jesus. Telling him that he was not my Lord, and in return He showed me mercy, rescuing me from the Abyss. I love my grandmother for praying me out of that place. I never want to see that again."

As the crowd dispersed, the enchanters vowed to change their lives, now grasping how blessed they were to accompany the Lord, equally terror-stricken by Victoria's experience, and consciously terror-stricken by their behavior in His presence.

The women eventually scheduled a meeting with Victoria's grandmother, on a pilgrimage to change their style of living.

With Joannes aboard, The Devotees persevered to the Mission Inn Hotel for forty winks, before heading to Dallas Texas the next ante meridiem. After morning arrived and everyone was fully groomed, Yeshua and His appointees entered into the mobile home, prepared for a lengthy journey to Dallas Texas. Before leaving Dallas the sovereignty headed to Wal-Mart on Van Buren Boulevard for food and other necessities. Kirtana, Olympia, Rachelle, and Shanese created a separate enumeration containing items suggested from a different Devotee.

While waiting for the ladies, Shawn heard a knock on the front door of the Elemment Palazzo. When Shawn opened the door, an able-bodied Caucasian thug with tattoos and a bold head forced himself inside the vehicle. "This is a pickpocket rendezvous, between me and everybody's pocket," the man states pulling out a STI Eagle. "Now anybody who thinks about moving will be the newest murder statistic."

Pointing the gun against Shawn's torso, the thug forces everyone to the back. "Oh I knew it was somebody much-publicized in this spacecraft," the thug states when he ogles Faye O. "Give it up pop star before you get popped." Everyone cooperates while the thug rummages the mobile home. Looking at Faye O's shirt the thug states, "What does your shirt say? 'Jesus loves me' Yea Jesus loves me too, that's the reason people cheerfully give me their belongings. Now take that shirt off and bra, I have been waiting to watch a sex tape of you, ha-ha."

Faye O hesitantly pulls up her shirt. When the bottom hem was just above her belly button the thug suddenly falls to his knees with Yeshua walking up from behind. "I have been on earth a week and witnessed two robberies. One was too many," Yeshua stated, now standing in front of the thug.

Aghast the thug bows, worshiping before Yeshua's feet. Abruptly the thug looks up; Yeshua stares into his dilated pupils and states, "Murdock, this is the last day you destroy a temple of the Holy Spirit. Now your synagogue is of Satan, for you knew I loved thee." Murdock slowly fell to his death. When Kirtana, the Olive sisters, and Rachelle returned to the Elemment Palazzo, cops flooded the scene along with an ambulance. After determining Murdock died from a heart attack the cops allowed the Devotees to leave.

Kirtana, the Olive sisters, and Rachelle alternated on the expressway averaging five and a half driving hours a piece. After arriving in Dallas Texas, the Devotees stayed at the Rosewood Mansion on Turtle Creek for forty winks, before wandering throughout Dallas for the next Devotee.

When ante meridiem flourished, Yeshua and His appointees walked towards the mobile home. In the hotel's lobby Rachelle noticed a quondam member of her ex-boyfriend's church. Ecstatic to see her, Rachelle approached the woman to engage in a conversation.

"I don't know if you remember me, but I had to come and speak," Rachelle states, interested in discovering whether Pastor Booker followed Yeshua's instructions.

"Hey! Of course I remember you. You're Pastor Booker's ex-lady," the parishess†[05] stated, showing genuine interest in the conversation. "You were a great woman of God and Pastor was silly to let you go."

"Thank you," Rachelle responds with a smile. "I only attended on a couple of occasions but I recognized you because your prayers were so powerful. So what church do you attend presently?"

"Well ... believe it or not, I'm back at New Temple Community Church with Pastor Booker. And you won't believe it but we have service on the Sabbath," the parishess stated.

"Girl that is awesome, what made you go back?" Rachelle

---

05. [par-i-shsis] a female member in a local church.

responds, vaguely persist in uncovering whether Pastor Booker followed Yeshua's edification; not interested romantically, but knowing his value in the kingdom.

"He came and hunted me down and apologized to everyone he ran off. I know it should be about God and not man, but my faith was so broken after that situation." the parishess stated with passion.

"Yes it is about God, but I can understand where you are coming from," Rachelle stated, glancing back at the Elemment Palazzo parked outside. "Well it was nice talking to you girl. I have got to go, but I will definitely see you soon."

"Likewise, it was nice talking to you," the parishess states as Rachelle offers a hug before departing.

When Rachelle enters the mobile home, slightly hesitant, she offers a recommendation for the next destination. After Yeshua agrees, Kirtana heads to the convenience store to fill up with Texas Tea. When at the pump, a dispossessed gentleman scrounged Kirtana for a dollar to purchase nourishment. Unable to provide cash due to the station's broken ATM, the man took offense.

"I know you have the cash look at the vehicle you are riding in," the man hostilely stated with a Redneck Drinkers Accent.

Kirtana took offense as well due to the man's disposition but humbly responds, "Yeeea, I do have it but the stores ATM is broken and I can't remove any cash at the moment. Sorry Sir."

"Yea I hear you. I don't know why I asked. You Latins and Blacks are all the same," the man responds.

Kirtana, stunned in the man response, replies, "Excuse me."

Yeshua walks up to the man and states, "Jock, you are a man of great faith, and you pray faithfully, but I have one complaint. You only love those who are Caucasian. What if you went to heaven and Jesus was black? Would you reject Him?" Jock Garth turned around slightly glazing at Yeshua's bronze arms and slowly beheld He's fiery lamp optics†⁰⁶ as Yeshua continued, "The woman that you disrespected is my Vice President, an individual that I hand-picked. I was thinking of selecting you as my new Devotee. Are you saying that I have a distorted judge of character?" Jock holds his head down in shame as Yeshua continues, "Do not judge others, and you will not be judged. For you will be treated as you treat others. The standard you use in judging is the standard by which you will be judged."

Too embarrassed to remain in Yeshua's presence Jock walks away with his head still tilted. As Jock departs, Kirtana responds in an undoubtedly facetious manner, "You give up to easy Redneck."

Jock, noticing Kirtana's forgiveness through humor, runs over to embrace her, "I still have not forgiving myself, so I am further ashamed for your forgiveness," Jock stated, immediately walking over to Yeshua, bowing at his feet. "Is that offering still on the table my Lord?" Jock asks Yeshua while showing reverence.

Yeshua smiles replying, "Welcome," and everyone entered the Elemment Palazzo.

Switching positions, Rachelle drove back to the Rosewood Mansion while Kirtana revealed Jock's position as an agriculturalist, and explained the objectives of the Devotees. Arriving at the Rosewood, Jock was escorted by Kirtana, as they vocally skylarked amongst one another while heading to the room. After he was well groomed, Jock was provided a Brooks Brothers suit from the Dallas Fashion Squad. With Kirtana and Jock back in the mobile home, Rachelle finally headed to their destination for the next Devotee.

Along the way Rachelle turned to a hit talk radio station

06. Daniel 10:6

in Dallas. Predestinately, Pastor Booker made a guest appearance on the airwaves and spoke about assisting to remove gangbangers from the street: providing spiritual guidance for the adults and becoming a theosire†⁰⁷ to the youth. Pastor Booker also spoke about his encounter with Yeshua. When speaking about his encounter with Yeshua the radio personality strangely became more interested in the interview:

"So Pastor Booker, are you saying that Jesus is here now?" the radio personality stated with sarcasm.

"Yes He is, and anyone not living for Him does not have much time left," stated Pastor Booker.

"Much time left?" the radio personality responds with chuckles, finding gaiety in making a mockery out of the Second Advent. Pastor Booker's discomfort became obvious over the airwaves as he remained silent. "Come-on, let's keep it de facto Pastor Booker, you know Emmanuelists†⁰⁸ have been claiming Jesus was coming since my grandmother nursed on a bottle. Emmanuelists have claimed the world was coming to an end at the end of the twentieth century and nothing happened then. Don't you think this is getting a bit redundant by now?" giggling the radio personality finishes, "Come-on Pastor Booker."

To revamp his anger Pastor Booker chuckles and states, "It is not my responsibility to muscle any being to believe: Jesus is a man of freewill. I'm just a harbinger."

"I hear feces, I hear feces. No disrespect Pastor, no disrespect. On the next topic, I heard your ministry was in danger of closing indefinitely due to members leaving. How did you get them to come back?" quoted the New Aged radio personality.

Laughing Pastor Booker states, "I'd rather not go into details due to obvious reasons unbeknownst to you, but let's just

---

07. [thee-uh-sahyuhr] a man who practices sacred paternal care over other person(s); a spiritual father
08. [ih-man-yoo-uhl-list] a person who believes in Jesus Christ: God with us

say I received celestial advice that enabled me to convince them into returning."

While listening to the live show, Yeshua instructed Rachelle to drive to the station in which Pastor Booker spoke, and after arriving, they all waited outside for Pastor Booker to depart after the interview. Several minutes transpired as Pastor Booker exited the station schlepping towards his vehicle. Tout de suite, a femme fatale approached Pastor Booker with the intent of seducing him with her beauteous semblance. Noticing that her gestures were ineffectual due to Pastor Bookers yeshuanity,†⁰⁹ the coquette convinced Booker to become her escort for "safety reasons," en route to her vehicle; midway, the femme fatale pulled Booker closer for a diversion to elicit a gun.

In the bitsy journey of approaching the coquette's vehicle, Yeshua—meticulously walking behind her and Booker from the point of departure—states, "Belinda! Get out of her!" Suddenly the femme fatale provided a slight jerk, releasing Pastor Booker, looking at the gun in disorientation. Embarrassed due to her possession of the firearm she replies, "Huh," suddenly the enchantress was shaken by the feeling of another presence.

After her volte-face, Yeshua looks into her eyes states, "Francia, I know you are confused as to why you are here to murder Pastor Booker. And I tell you, stop entertaining evil spirits through music and extracurricular activities involving insobriety, tricking for the prostitute. Be sober-minded; be watchful. Your adversary the devil prowls around like a roaring lion, seeking someone to devour. Follow the advice of your father who prays for your salvation; for I will not be amongst you long."

Pastor Booker was blithe to catch sight of Yeshua on another occasion, pleasantly requisitioning Francia for the gun. Knowing who confronted her, Francia was sheepish in toto,

---

09. [yosh-oo-an-i-tee] having or possessing characteristics of Christ through the Holy Spirit or a personnel encounter.

handing Pastor Booker the gun before bowing at Yeshua's feet. "S'il vous plaît pardonnez-moi Jésus," Francia stated, pleading for Jesus to forgive her in the language that she spoke as a child, recalling her father's worship growing up in France. Yeshua accepted her atonement and offered His hand pulling her to her feet, and in that instant she walked away a femme vital.†[10]

Without wasting any time Yeshua interacts with Pastor Booker, "I am impressed with your obedience. Not only have your members returned to Christ, but you have pointed more nonbelievers towards the light. But still you are not confident in the Spirit. You hear my voice but cannot completely separate it from Satan who also speaks. Be one of my Devotees and I will teach you the discernment needed for you to advance," Yeshua states in a Many Oceans Dialect.

Pastor Booker stares with puzzlement concerned about his followers, "I am not worthy to be in your presence my Deity so I will most definitely accept your overture. Although I am confused, do my sermons contain any blasphemies?" Pastor Booker asks.

"The Holy Spirit fully operates within your sermons, but discernment is needed after you leave the lectern," Yeshua responds.

Subsequent, Yeshua and Pastor Booker enter the Elemment Palazzo, and Rachelle travels back to the Rosewood Mansion for forty winks; before traveling to Miami Florida the next ante meridiem. After cockcrow, everyone, well groomed, entered the mobile home on their journey to Miami Florida. Shawn, Joannes, Jock and Pastor Booker alternated on the expressway averaging five and a half driving hours a piece.

The temperature described why Miami's NBA team was named Heat, as the Devotees drove through Magic City in tran-

---

10. [fem-vahyt-l] a beautiful woman inside and out; an exquisite woman physically, one who fears God

sit to temporary habitation. Kirtana made reservations at a Presidential Villa, and provided Jock—the designated driver—with directions. When arriving at the luxury mansion the Devotees took forty winks, preparing for another pilgrimage.

At the birth of ante meridiem, Faye O was wakened by a knock on the door. Surprised by the visitor, Faye O ecstatically embraced Bay Girl—an old friend and dried up artist from the music industry.

"Like what are you doing here girl? I haven't seen you in ages," Faye O says giggling; noticing Bay Girl's constant and strange look over shoulder quirk, Faye O continues, "What's up with the straitjacket-act?"†[11]

"You know how it is, booking showings and selling out stadiums. You know how I do," Bay Girl says, now looking back sporadically—in order to make her nervousness less obvious—due to Faye O's commit.

"Yeeeea oo-k, are you alright girl?" Faye O says, still confused regarding Bay Girl's bizarre behavior. Suddenly an unmarked van pulls up and two men make off with Faye O and Bay Girl. In another room, Yeshua was made aware of the kidnapping through the Spirit of Truth, and rouse Kirtana in pursuit of the body snatchers.

The gloved body snatchers drive to an undisclosed area and exchange vans, forcing Faye O in the cargo area and allowing Bay Girl to accompany them in the passenger seat. The confessing malefactors head to the Banyan Tree Seychelles and along the way Faye O overhears the powwow. Bay Girl, starting to reconsider, reveals herself as an accomplice; while the body snatchers reminded her that Faye O had to be sacrificed to Baal in order for her to regain fame and fortune. Faye O, hurt by the betrayal of her close friend began to weep, but her heart was shortly strengthened by the faith of Yeshua's soon approaching.

11. [streyt-jak-it-akt] the act of displaying strange mannerisms; weird behavior

While Kirtana drove through Miami, Yeshua prayed—searching within—as the Spirit of Truth manifested Faye O's location. After arriving at the destination, Yeshua attempted to enter a social gathering involving affiliates of the entertainment industry. The gathering was located at the Banyan Tree Seychelles in a Presidential Villa—blueprinted for the dwelling of a king. Yeshua was rudely stopped at the door by a bouncer who asked for his name, checking a list.

Yeshua states, "I am here for one of my Devotees, my name is not of importance in regards to your list. Like many of the names on your list are not of importance in the book of life."

Unexpectedly there was a loud scream, and two men ran out of the swimming pool area holding Faye O, placing her on the floor to perform CPR. The rich and famous stared with indifference but continued the soiree, while Yuhann Shareef—a preeminent up and coming actor—continued to perform CPR. After many tries Yuhann loses hope as the media announced the famous pop star dead at the age of twenty one. An outraged Yuhann expresses his feelings in an Arabic Accent forthwith, "Why is there a party when a human life is in need of assistance? Are you people zombies!? Do you have an essence, or is it all about facwad?†[12] For what shall it profit a man, if he shall gain the whole world, and lose his own soul? And now you look confused probably asking yourselves. 'Is that a quote from one of his new movies?' No! It's from the word of God Almighty, but maybe that's the problem; you are too busy worshiping Benjamin. I am in the wrong business, you people are sickening."

As Yuhann begins to walk towards the exit, Yeshua looks into his eyes and states, "I am impressed by your choice of words Yuhann and I tell you, Ianto Crunn and you are excluded from this statement, but videotape everything you see here and hereafter." Yeshua continues in a Loud Thundering Accent,

12. [fak-wod] to make rolls of money 2. cash, funds

"You have killed Faye O though sacrifice therefore officially she belongs to Me. For I have the final say in where her soul will be. I Am the Great I Am, King of Kings, King of your Satan who dwells within your temple. For the bodies you have sacrificed, you will not go unpunished. For the days you have mocked God willfully promoting Satan, you will not go unpunished. And your judgment is within this hour. While you bow and confess that I, Jesus Christ am Lord, you still will not be saved; for you were not grateful for sight so remain darkness. Now that you see that I am real, and now believe, it is too late. You have denied me and now I deny you. You will not die today but will await the first terror, which is soon to come."

After bowing, every Idol shared a demeanor of emptiness money could not fill, captured on camera for the world to witness. There was a moment of silence, as if the famous paid tribute to someone of their own, now resting in peace; not aware that a tribute was paid for their soul. To break the silence Yeshua says, "Faye O, get up my Devotee you are now free! Yuhann and Ianto, you are my ninth and tenth Devotees," Yeshua looks the bouncer in the eyes as He continues, "You three are the only souls of importance on this gatherings list that are of importance in the book of life."

The rich and famous were in awe as they witnessed Faye O rise from the dead. Bay Girl provided a stare unlike any of the other superstars, realizing the cold-heartedness of her betrayal, especially now, absorbing that the sacrifice was all in vain. Yuhann gathered the camera equipment, offering the director over the amount of funds to cover the loss. The discouraged director rejected the money, temporary replacing mammon with an awareness of the true and living God; afterwards Yeshua, Ianto, and Faye O walked outdoors to enter the Elemment Palazzo. Some of the lionized remained on their knees while others wondered haphazardly, but all participated in an identical vacant stare. When Yuhann exited he noticed the soulless room and shook his head with sympathy.

While waiting outside in the mobile home, Kirtana heard the news of Faye O's death and began to break into deep prayer. Shortly witnessing Faye O exit the party Kirtana screamed, "Hallelujah," embracing her blissfully as she entered with Yeshua and the two new Devotees. When Yeshua and Kirtana made their reoccurrence at the Presidential Villa, the apprehensive Devotees broke into genuflection, witnessing Faye O exit the Elemment Palazzo. After Yuhann and Ianto were introduced as the two new Devotees, the genuflection flourished into innocuous regalement, as Yeshua and His enthusiast celebrated life.

Following the celebration, everyone took forty winks to prepare for a vagabondage to Chicago Illinois. After sun rose on South Beach, everyone entered the mobile home. Shawn, Joannes, Jock, Pastor Booker and Ianto alternated on the expressway averaging three driving hours a piece. When arriving in The Windy City, Ianto drove to The Palmer House Hilton for temporary dwelling.

When entering His room Yeshua noticed a group of approximately ten men—all with ruffian characteristics—enter a room near the end of the hallway. Suddenly The Spirit of Truth revealed activities in which the privately infamous minxist†[13] entertained. The minxist/jezebel was a canonized and well-respected Judge in Chicago Illinois: due to her unsparing but equitable judgments. As the female Devotees entered their rooms, numerous thugs approached the Jezebel's room. Surprisingly the thugs were respectful, reframing from cajoling the Olive sisters as one stated "Excuse me Ma'am", progressing adjacent to the siblings—who are both extremely stunning women. Yeshua remained in the hallway telling Kirtana and the Devotees to rest, in preparation to search for the last two Devotees.

Simultaneously furnishing sacred writings, Yeshua min-

13. [mingks-ist] a woman who believes in whoredom; a sexually promiscuous female

istered to every fornicator as they exited the Judges room for the night. After successfully proselytizing every adulterer, Yeshua noticed the Judge exit her room with one last adulterer. After they passed Yeshua, He watched with uneasiness until they left His sight, thereafter He enters Ianto and Yuhann's room to dwell for forty winks, settling for the next morning.

The next ante meridiem brought promise beyond imagination, as the Devotees socialized for brunch at the Lockwood Restaurant, two souls closer to supremacy. The Judge glances while passing Yeshua, Kirtana, and the current Devotees—specifically noticing Kirtana and Yeshua, and promptly settled at a nearby table; casually the Judge holds her head down in shame. South State Street was the next landing place as Yeshua and His enthusiast entered the mobile home. When approaching South State Street, The Spirit of Truth revealed to Yeshua a cataclysmic meeting held in the Downtown Islamic Center—a meeting occupied by Belial and his Abeyance. Yeshua suggested for Kirtana to park the mobile home in a secluded area as He prayed, mobilizing for the troubles ahead.

A woman outside of the building spoke with a bullhorn, preaching the truth about Jesus and the deception of the Muslim religion: "The Quran's Allah is not God Almighty in the Holy Bible. Do not be deceived my people. Allah is described as the best deceiver, schemer, or planner. Don't take my word for it read the Quran's text. The greatest deceiver in The Holy Bible is known as Satan. Open your eyes and turn towards The Light, which is Jesus Christ. The truth is the truth, so notice you will find Jesus in the Quran but will not find Mohammad or Allah in the Holy Bible. Why is this? (Because the Holy Bible existed first?)No, because the great deceiver tells half of the truth, but God Almighty cannot lie," the woman preaches speaking in an Arabic Accent.

A soldier of the Abeyance over hears the disrespect towards Belial—disrespect due to Belial's undercover Muslim faith, acting as an Emmanuelist—and acts as a stool pigeon by interrupting the meeting to inform Belial about the woman's preachment. Insightful of the current dangers, Yeshua exits the mobile home telling Kirtana and the Devotees to wait in the vehicle.

While both events transpire the woman concurrently continues to preach, "Now I will not quote the Quran by speaking the deceiver's words in the atmosphere and disrespect Jehovah, but I will explain the awe-inspiringly compelling yet twisted text. The Quran inveigles the mind, deceivingly promoting homosexually in Suras 52:22-28. The hypocrisy reads between verses 22nd through the 28th. First the passage states that men will drink and socialize without sin. Immediately afterwards, Allah offers virgin boys—hidden pearls—to men as a reward for making it to Paradise. The men will be relieved when the virgin boys are offered, because their families have told them that homosexuality was wrong in Allah's eyes. Then they will think to themselves 'I used to pray for deliverance but Allah allows us to sin when in Paradise, not throwing us in everlasting flame; he is so "merciful",' this is blasphemy. I have homosexual friends that I have attempted to usher to The Light, you know. I do not judge them but I must tell the truth for their own salvation. It is sin, as well as killing, fornication, lying, among others which are all equal; and will not be allowed in heaven. The planner is a lie."

Portraying Himself as one of her listeners, Yeshua suddenly looks into the woman eyes and states, "Yana you are one of my most faithful and the career you sacrificed for my honor did not go unnoticed. Now hurry, get into the mobile home before your eyes; we have little time left." Recognizing who confronted her, Yana Obi follows the Lord's request as the Spirit of Truth revealed the blessing before her eyes—the secluded area in which the Elemment Palazzo was parked—and entered into the sovereignty just as Belial and five soldiers from the Abeyance exited the Islamic Center. First confused, but shortly grasping that Yeshua replaced the woman preacher/teacher Belial feels threatened by his campaigns competition.

"We intersect yet again," Belial states after the soldiers cock their shotguns pointing at Yeshua. The soldiers' formation resembled a crescent moon with Belial in the middle like a star. "Your quintessence is engendering dilemma beyond my expectations. I except self-condemnation for acquiescing you to insufflate, but now I authorize your obliteration." The soldiers attempt to discharge their weapons but every gun jams.

While the soldiers attempted to fire again Yeshua states, "You are confused in your authority, for I do not fall subject to this world, but the world to me." Suddenly the guns were removed from the soldiers' hands, now pointing towards Belial and the five soldiers. While the weapons divorced Belial and the soldiers, seraphim were gradually revealed, becoming more visible as they approached Yeshua. When in Yeshua's presence the seraphim formation resembled a cross, and from Belial's perspective the cross appeared sideways. The five seraphim provided armed reinforcement while standing onward in relation to Yeshua: One seraph positioned to His left, another in His immediate front, accompanying two on His right, and the last—to be more than first—stood onward of the second seraph.

Dismayed by the supernatural event, a speechless Belial smirked revealing malice, recognizing his inability to tyrannize Yeshua. Dysfunctional in his current locale, Belial holds up his hands. To the naked eye, it would seem that his gesture of surrender was due to the guns pointed in his direction. However the gesture was a form of intimidation: in an attempt to capture the attention of the Secret Service. When the Secret Service recognized Belial's beckon from a distance, they called for backup from other secret agents and soldiers in the Abeyance. After calling for reinforcement, the secret agents attempt to shoot the effulgently miraculous cross formation, but experiencing Abeyance déjà vu their guns jammed in like modus operandi.

The Spirit of Truth revealed more soldiers were en route; therefore Yeshua quickly entered the Elemment Palazzo to avoid endangering Kirtana or any of the Devotees. When entering the vehicle, Yeshua provided Kirtana with the next destination; afterwards, He walked into the master bedroom for prayer. About ten minutes elapse as Kirtana drove towards the Palmer House Hilton. While switching lines she noticed a vehicle following: insistently tailgating one car behind. To avoid paranoia, Kirtana performed a U-turn that was by sight deceptively venturous— but in actuality a cautious move into the opposite direction, and thereupon the tailgater made a U-turn confirming Kirtana's intuition.

No longer demonstrating discreetness, the driver directly tailgates Kirtana and the Devotees while Yeshua continued to pray. Suddenly the pursuer initiated strobe lights and sounded a Yelp siren, revealing the tailgaters identity—law enforcement. Yeshua's prayer was interrupted by the siren, and immediately, He walked towards the passenger area to obtain vindication for the inquiry. When Kirtana pulled over, the cops ordered her to exit and place her hands on the vehicle. After following the law of the land, cop one patted Kirtana down and casually asked for permission to search the vehicle.

"We received word that you were harboring a fugitive," cop two states as his partner searched Kirtana.

"A fugitive!?" Kirtana pseudowitlessly†[14] responds; unwilling to give up Yeshua. "There is no one in this vehicle that has the thought of a desire to commit a crime."

"I hear you Ma'am, but do you mind if we search your vehicle?" cop one requested again as he finished searching Kirtana.

"Should I let them search the vehicle Jesus?" Kirtana hails jocosely, looking up at Yeshua in the mobile home.

As Kirtana looked up at Yeshua in the window the cops

14. [soo-doh-wit-lis-lee] feign ignorance; the act of playing dumb

miscalculated the direction of her optics, concluding that she looked upon the heavens for an answer—taken her question as a form of spoof, not knowing that she literally asked Jesus a question in the mobile home. "Ma'am I don't appreciate the holy quip, you can let us search the vehicle now or you can wait here until we approve a search warrant. At that point this small issue will become much more extreme," cop two states in an aggressive manner.

Looking back at Yeshua once again Kirtana states, "I would like to apologize, Mr. Officer. You both can search as you please," providing an answer to the question and allowing the search after Yeshua's nod for approval.

The two detectives enter the mobile home and were accosted by Yeshua; immediately distinguishing Yeshua as the transgressor in question, cop one states, "Come with us sir," as Yeshua looked into his eyes. Suddenly the cop provided a stare of disquietude: due to fear caused by capturing Yeshua's wither. Well aware that guns were left on the scene cop one contravenes his own order and states, "If we are unable to find any guns from the crime scene, we have to let you go sir. We will not be of inconvenience long." Cop two looked at cop one with confusion, but after a look into Yeshua's eyes he avoided any questioning.

When searching the Elemment Palazzo the cops contemplated Faye O and were panic-stricken, thinking Faye O would recollect their last junction, the detectives stared at Faye O with their mouths open. "Hey, I am Faye O. How are you gentlemen this fine evening?" Faye O states with a Pseudo Unaware of Their Identity Mannerism. After the cops nod their heads down as a greeting, still in shock, the unsettled union concluded their investigation.

The two detectives walk towards the passenger seat to exit. "We did not find any wea-weapons so weee ... mmmust let you go, bbbut by orders we must arrest someone. So we will hold Miss Miguel in custody for reckless driving," cop one states with a slight stammer.

Yeshua looked into both men eyes one by one and states, "You wonder why Faye O does not know your identity, and I tell you, her forgiveness is mistaken for ignorance. Faye O knows your evil ways and so do I. Kirtana is my Vice President and no harm will come upon her. If one hair is broken from her crown I will show no mercy. Now be still, while I converse with my appointee."

Yeshua whispers in Kirtana's ear a message of significance. Although the message was serious it also brought about a comforting smile to her countenance; a message partially guaranteeing that she would experience no manhandling. Afterwards, the detectives took Kirtana to Cook County Jail. Subsequently the Devotees bailed Kirtana out, whose bond was a ridiculous one million dollars, due a solicitation from Belial. The Devotees avoided the Palmer House Hilton to keep a low profile until Kirtana's court date the next morning; booking a room at the Waldorf Astoria Chicago in Jock's name: the Devotee whose national status was less notable.

Morning tide arose as Yeshua and the Devotees spruced up for Kirtana's court date. Shawn provided his legal advice, lacking a license to practice law in Chicago Illinois, therefore unable to represent Kirtana. Shawn forewarned Yeshua and his Kindred-in-Christ that Kirtana would need a lawyer; putting emphasis on the outrageous quotation of the bail set for a simple reckless driving charge. Shawn concludes that due to Belial's dictator authority it was a great possibility that a charge other and/or more severe than reckless driving was added to the case. Kirtana motioned that she would plead her own case, and rely on The Holy Spirit to change the heart of the appointed Judge: Joana Villa.

After arriving at the courthouse Yeshua instructed Faye O to serve as a witness in Kirtana's defense. When entering the private courtroom with Kirtana and Shawn, Faye O instantly realized why Yeshua recommended her to be a witness, as she observed on a third occasion the cops that were responsible for her body snatching. Also present was Belial: the Commander in Chief; along with the four soldiers that accompanied him at the Downtown Islamic Center. Before court began the district attorney asked Kirtana the details of her representation and how she wanted to plea.

One cop yells, "All rise! Court is in-session the honorable Judge Villa now residing," just as Judge Villa enters the courtroom, following, "You may be seated," when she settled. After the completion of arranging documents Judge Villa states:

"This is case number 31C01-1212-CR-00763, in the matter of Kirtana Miguel. Present in the court room is the defendant Miss Miguel and she will represent herself in this case. The right of a jury has been waived due to orders of Belial: the Commander in Chief of Columbia. Therefore all evidence of attempted murder following reckless driving will be presented to me for ruling. The defendant will be cross-examined conjointly with witnesses that were present that evening. How does the defendant plea?"

Following Judge Villa's opening statement, ten seconds passed as Shawn and Faye O glanced at one another with entanglement. Kirtana leered back at Shawn and Faye O with a similar reaction, discomposed apropos of the attempted murder charge.

"Miss Miguel how do you plea?" Judge Villa repeats with disaffection, expressing her impatience.

"Not guilty Your Honor," Kirtana states with restfulness as The Spirit of Truth instantly settled upon her, creating confidence in her plea.

"Please continue," Judge Villa states providing a downward head gesture.

"Well Your Honor, I was off of E Jackson Drive speaking

to a ruffian kid named Daquan P., I'm not sure of his last name. He stated that he remembered me from the Palmer House Hilton. He went on to explain his rendezvous with an important figure of the law ..."

Judge Villa interrupts Kirtana, banging her gavel aggressively, "Order, order, what does Mr. Price have to do with this case Miss Miguel?" noticing Kirtana's flummoxed stare in reaction to her conniption, Judge Villa previously suspected but now doubted Kirtana's use of blackmail. In addition, the Judge realized that she divulged Daquan's surname. Foot in her mouth, she called for a recess, summoning Kirtana and Belial into a private room.

When entering the room Belial fleetly states, "Where is the ringleader of your organization? You are ineffectual to me."

Kirtana looks at Belial with confidence, simpers and replies, "I plead the fifth."

"Have you hypothesized that I stimulate derision? What a fool you are unequivocally. I seize supremacy to reap the benefits from your life insurance; and you mock me?"

"You have no authority over me; I am a child of The Most High," Kirtana ends with a chuckle.

"Enough you two, if I didn't know any different I would think you two were married," Judge Villa states promptly throwing advances at Belial, "So, Belial, do you have a case against this young lady? Or is her presence an example of you exercising your authority?" Belial is entertained by the Judges enticement taking his sagacity slave.

"I have no dealings with her. I am interested in her ringleader," Belial states, dumbing his speech due to his interest in Judge Villa.

"Well I will take it from here Mr. Commander. Go home and get some rest, but call me before you completely close your eyes for the night. We will schedule a rendezvous to meet antecedent to meridiem."

"Will do," Belial states with his head in the clouds gently touching Judge Villa's arm: pioneering her bicep and harboring at her hand; just as he retired the private room.

Judge Villa stood to reposition, body following her eyes and eyes following Belial; waiting on him to leave along with four soldiers of the Abeyance. Judge Villa's quivering body cringed, promptly rolling her eyes with displeasure after realizing that Belial completely exited the courtroom, thereupon replying, "Ugh," unimpressed with his handsomeness.

"Now that situation is resolved, I will proceed to dismiss this case due to exculpatory evidence."

Kirtana smiled, remembering what Yeshua whispered in her ear, having faith that His promise would come to past: resulting in a dismissal of her life changing criminal charges. In her mind she screamed Hallelujah while Judge Villa continued to speak.

"I know this next question may resemble unprofessionalism in a court environment, but who was Belial referring to when mentioning your ringleader?"

Kirtana smiled again and states, "These are not my words and I have been left ignorant to your lifestyle, but if you really want to know Him, He said you have to change your ways."

Initially Judge Villa stares at Kirtana with a how-dare-you perplexity. Attempting to cover up her reaction with a false front, the Judge immediately makes an effort to befriend Kirtana and her Ringleader, "Why don't you and your ringleader attend a gathering of mine tonight? There will be food, entertainment, and many individuals of importance."

Kirtana characterized Judge Villa as a pseudologist, but in an attempt to introduce her to Christ and save her soul she accepted Judge Villa's invitation, "It would be an honor. We will see you there."

Judge Villa was startled in Kirtana's answer, conscious that her invitation appeared insincere. After Judge Villa provided the gatherings location, the two exchanged information. Subsequently, Kirtana left the courthouse with her Kindred-in-Christ and entered the Elemment Palazzo. While Yeshua prayed the Devotees gave ovation, grateful that Kirtana was emancipated with no criminal charges.

Later that evening, Kirtana conversed with Yeshua at the Lockwood Restaurant to confirm whether accepting Judge Villa's invitation was the right decision; while the Devotees entered their rooms to get dressed, waiting for the next destination.

"My Deity, I felt Judge Villa had the traits of a highbinder, however in Spirit I also felt obligated to respond 'Yes' to her invitation. Thinking just maybe, she would change her ways," Kirtana states with inquisitiveness.

Yeshua smiles and responds with a Many Oceans Accent, "You were not mistaken when you heard my voice as a response. Remember you are a good judge of character. This is one of the reasons you are my Vice President."

Following Yeshua's carte blanche to attend the soiree, after sunset, Yeshua and His appointees drove to a private airport in which the gathering was held. The congregate was in celebration of Judge Villa's membership at Zephyr and Seven Seas—a club consisting of only yacht and plane owners. The Judge's membership was authentic due to her recent investment in a private plane named Largesse™ in which Judge Villa made known was designated after her interest in selfhood, bestowing upon herself a gift. Before entering the occasion Yeshua spoke with the Devotees to avoid any spiritual deviate.

"There will be dangers at this gathering but do not be afraid; for we are children of The Father and fear is not within our characteristics. We will not participate in any meaningless activities or conversations; for engaging in these with sinners can lead to sin. Our mission is always to save souls; you must understand this is our only reason for attending. There will be people of importance at this gathering, but our purpose is not to network; for we are well connected in God's kingdom," **Yeshua** states in a Many Ocean Accent.

Since Kirtana had an invitation, the Devotees and their true Shepherd followed, as she made sure everyone was clear to attend. When everyone entered the terminal, each Devotee was approached by an attendant or two, recognizing them from their past profession. Judge Villa noticed Kirtana with Yeshua—identifying Him as the ringleader, and made a suspiciously prompt phone call before announcing herself.

"What a night," Judge Villa states as an introduction after quickly ending her call, revealing a clandestine demeanor. "Are you going to introduce me to your friend Kirtana?"

"I think it would be more appropriate if He introduced himself," Kirtana responds; suddenly two ruffian men dressed in suits scurried up to Yeshua and bowed.

"I fell short again," one man states following the other:

"I need help, please!" the repenters plead for forgiveness.

Judge Villa provided a peculiar stare as she witnessed the men bow at Yeshua's feet. Yeshua whispers in both of their ears, knowing the men's embarrassment for falling short once again. One of the men notices Kirtana, and quickly holds his head down in shame after eye contact; the other man states, "We have to talk," directing his statement towards Judge Villa.

With the identical peculiar stare now directed at Yeshua and Kirtana, Judge Villa states, "If you would excuse me for a moment. We will continue our discussion soon."

The two men walkaway while Judge Villa trailed behind. On the opposite side of the airports gate, the Olive sisters conversed with two successful doctors from Philadelphia. The doctors explained how they became business partners investing in Nurse Jubilee—a well-known yacht.

"I remember you two were considered the Mother of the streets in Philadelphia, providing parental guidance at a young age. As I recall you two turned teenagers' lives around in substantial multitudes. Where did you all go?" one doctor asks, beginning the conversation with a mannerism of professionalism, but ending with a semblance sarcasm.

"I heard the streets got the best out of them," the other doctor tells his partner with a smirk; both participating in an inside joke.

Shanese and Olympia smile at one another as they connect. "Yes I remember you, what is your name Dr. White. You are a great doctor, I bless God for you. I have definitely heard about all of the lives that you have saved; except for that one black kid who just needed foot surgery. Did he make it?" Shanese states with sarcasm.

Slightly cutting off Shanese's words Olympia states, "Dr. Castro is it? Awesome doctor, awesome doctor, but the story that I heard about refusing to do surgery on a black kid was troubling. I heard the awful story about the rape of your daughter. I'm sorry about that. What if I told you the white kid raped your daughter, and set up the black kid that tried to come to her aid. Would you have refused to perform surgery on the black kid? In which ultimately caused his death? You all's yacht should be called Dr. Triple K."

The two doctors provided a mannerism of bewilderment; wondering how the sisters knew about the two deaths—deaths that were without a doubt classified. "We are living in the last days. Hatred against other races will not get you into the gates of heaven," Shanese states ending the conversation. Afterwards the Olive sisters and additional Devotees walk toward Yeshua and Kirtana. Unexpectedly Judge Villa rushes up to Yeshua, bows at His feet and states:

"Please forgive me. I did not serve you after I got saved. I have falling short over a thousand times, and I am not worthy to be in your presence on a third occasion. However please, you all must come with me. I called Belial when you all first arrived. He is coming as we speak with soldiers from the Abeyance. We must leave quickly."

Judge Villa and her pilots escorted Yeshua and His Appointees to her private plane. Before entering the glass Jet Bridge, strobe lights and sirens sounded while soldiers from the Abeyance surrounded the airplane. "You are presently beleaguered. Any individual endeavoring in entering the aircraft will be eradicated," Belial states while the soldiers point their firearm towards the Jet Bridge.

Suddenly soldiers flood the airport's terminal with Belial, heading towards the Devotees. The members of Zephyr and Seven Seas were shaken as they approached, but in Judge Villa's ear Kirtana whispers, "Do not fear."

Without delay every soldier begin to hold their heart dropping to their knees and releasing their guns while Yeshua states, "Every knee will bow," now looking Belial in the eyes He repeats in a Thundering Accent, "Every knee!" Belial trying to thwart holds his chest, following a buckle in his knees. After several attempts to resist, Belial's body and mind capitulates, and Belial emits a grunting sound as he slowly performs genuflection.

Yeshua instructs the pilots, Judge Villa, Kirtana and the women Devotees to enter the plane; latterly instructing the male Devotees to gather weapons dropped from the soldiers, and place them in the Jet Bridge before boarding; excluding Yuhann who from the beginning recorded every moment. After every gun was transported into the Jet Bridge, Yeshua relieved the pain from the soldiers and states, "I Am the Great I Am, King of Kings, The One who died and rose again."

"Czar!" one soldier yells interrupting Yeshua, concerned about Belial's current euphoria.

Yeshua looks the soldier in the eyes, and holds his hand straight out, arm in a thirty decree angle forming an Obey salute—not to be confused with a Nazi Salute. The soldier swiftly holds his chest again, continuing to bow, "You see your commander did not respond, because this message falls on his death ears. Your ears are also death, but you will remember when it is too late. Your commander will tell those of no faith that he is The Truth; and they will believe. He will tell those of no faith that I am not coming, when you see me clear as day; and they will believe. When you hear these things, you will realize you made the wrong choice; but will find no light in the darkness. Seek what little light that you have left; for I will not be amongst you long."

The Abeyance and the remaining club members were discombobulated as Yeshua entered the plane. While preparing for takeoff, Yeshua walked towards a guilt-ridden Judge Villa. Unable to contain her spirits, she bows once again in Yeshua's presence, officially pleading for salvation. "As you bow at my feet you are delivered. For the most infamous ghouls flee when in my presence. I have noticed your pretense displayed for others regarding the investment of this plane; but I know it was for charity reasons. Follow me as the last Devotee, and no longer fall short from the glory of God." Judge Villa cries historically and accepts Yeshua's overture; hoping not only to be delivered but enraptured in regards her new mission in Christ.

Pilot at the wheel, soldiers outside of the plane continued to bow, mirroring the outline of the runway: ten on the left and ten on the right. Belial also remained on his knees displaying a form of weakness in the eyes of his soldiers. After the plane was in the air Belial gained control of his body proceeding to stand, looking to the atmosphere with a disgruntling stare, as the plane departed.

Clause 2
The Third Temple

Ere One Thousand Two Hundred and Sixty Days

The Largesse™ landed at a secret location in Washington District of Columbia. Belial and The Abeyance were in pursuit of Yeshua and His appointees, but the American's Most Wanted list was not an option. Due to Belial's haughtiness he wanted the Yeshua controversy to appear frivolous in the eyes of The Abeyance. Eventually Belial treated his confrontations with Yeshua as mythology, starting by appraising the encounters low-ranking in comparison to the quickly approaching presidential election.

Relying on Belial's arrogance, Yeshua discerned the coast was clear; therefore Kirtana booked a luxury tour bus to escort them to Kirtana's mansion. Kirtana relentlessly kept in touch with her kids—who were under the benevolent care of her grandmother Jana—throughout the cavalcade to find the twelve Devotees; overly festive to be in their presence and concurrently insouciant knowing that her children's future president would change the world. Kirtana's festiveness could have been mistaken for indifference compared to her grandmother's festiveness towards Yeshua, immediately bowing to her knees, weeping. Afterwards Kirtana's grandmother apologized to Kirtana, subconsciously thinking that she ran off with a wealthy man for a romantic affair.

Yeshua went into another room to pray with Jana, while Kirtana allocated the Devotees future endeavors. Kirtana disclosed that each Devotee will have fifty representatives under them called Geotic-Virtues, endogenously dwelling in every state throughout Land of Liberty. Each Devotee will be provided with insight to create wonders in which could only be obtained from God Almighty Himself to past along to their Geotic-Virtues: more advanced than the wonders provided in Egypt. Since a thousand years is like one day according to God Almighty's abilities, the twelve Devotees combined would have the ability to restore and enrich the world's economy within three years. In conclusion, after the Devotees and their Geotic-Virtues display their wondrous abilities within Columbia, the fifty Geotic-Virtues will be the vanguards of fifty additional representatives each called The Geotic, and they would evolve universally.

After Kirtana divulged Yeshua's divine contrivance, the Devotees provided some of their own resources. Since Kirtana's mansion had an abundance of land, the Devotees engineered a runway and lighthouse for The Largesse™; they also invested in another plane named Almsgiver™. A top of the line studio was built for music and movie production. Advanced and undetectable communications through cell phones were created, along with similar internet connections. All of the Devotees invested in an online bank also undetectable by Columbia satellites. Finally a radio mast was engineered delivering Class I-A clear channel frequencies, as well as a Broadcasting Station; in addition to a high powered undetectable spacecraft satellite— dubbed MusaSatellite, and broadcasting antenna: all far more advanced than any on earth.

<u>One Thousand Two Hundred and Sixty Days</u>: prophetically: A vision provided by Lord Yeshua to His Appointees: Television programs across Columbia and the world delivered a special news report announcing that Belial won the election, and will be given two inauguration speeches: both in locations soon to be announced. Before the first speech, Yeshua informed

the Devotees of the revelations ahead, "The coming events will fulfill prophecies from the sacred text. The antichrist will perform miracles from the sky, created by a Power Plant in Egypt Giza's Great Pyramid. Many unbelievers and some believers will be fooled. The believers will turn towards me, and some unbelievers will then wonder if I exist. Followers of the antichrist will rejoice; and followers of the antichrist will be concerned; but both will be regretful when I come from the sky with my Seraphim. All will bow and call me King of Kings and Lord of Lords, wishing that I would now show mercy. Any man that takes the mark of the beast will completely deny me. What a sad day it will be for them. If believers lack faith they also could be in danger of taking the mark of the beast. The good news is you my Devotees will know the truth as Satan speaks. And hope will dwell upon unbelievers as they refuse the mark of the beast to turn towards The Light."

As Yeshua simplified Belial's forthcoming speech, Belial prepared to deliver his inveigled confabulate; infamously accomplished by political nomenclature interfusion: mixing complex vocabulary or jargon within his speech to confuse the masses. Kirtana, Grandma Jana, and the Devotees watched casually, only to observe Belial's choice of words. The revealing of one of the locations was not surprising as Columbia introduced Belial from Egypt Giza. Belial wasted no time uncovering the sphinx of the title New World:

"All of your predictions were authentic. Columbia's government is the Illuminati, but what authority do you acquire to terminate the inevitable. We are preponderate aloft every country of the terrene, so where will you eschew? What Divine Being will come to your rescue? Christ? Your Christ is not coming; I am Christ, for you have perceived the miracles in which I have effectuated. I am the King of Kings, for you perceive that I am the commander in chief, in a world abounding of Kings. I am the truth, for you perceive me clear as day, and no Divine Being will emerge from the celestial sphere. I have interchanged the Identification Card with a microchip. One can implant the microchip in the right hand, or if by cataclysm that limp has been anatomized, the forehead. Money is void, therefore all endowments are applied on the microchip, transferred from earth's solitary bank, and that bank will not acknowledge any personage without Identification. Any personage that cannot be identified cannot acquire or even apply for employment. I have fabricated a statue, if anyone renounces worship to my statue their microchip will be surceased; until it is proven that individual has obtained a vicissitude of cardiac organ." **Belial raises his hands and continues in his Lion Accent,** "Now, welcome to the Novus Ordo Seclorum; undeniably distinguished as The New World Order."

While Belial performs the Raising Hands Gesture,†[01] hot and cold impalpable beams emitted from the pyramid pointing towards the clouds forming a tornado and lighting. The tornado headed towards Belial as he raised his hands. Slightly lifted vertically from the ground, Belial lowers his hands and the tornado dematerialized before it had a chance to sweep him abroad. Belial continues his speech after the dissimulating weather display:

"Like a prophet I apperceive prospective occurrences, but contradictorily enlightenment is disclosed through my inner omnipotence. This explains the twister's demolishment, equiponderating the miracle spoken before its occurrence. What other Absolute Being but Christ could dehumidify a twister by bestowing extremity pantomimes. As I perorate, denizens across the spheroid petition for an alternate sovereign, and I will serve as the global mediator," **Belial ends in his Lion Accent.**

Suddenly the spotlight in which Belial manifested his well-cloaked performance blackened. Following the crowds "aw"

---

01. [rey-zing-handz-jes-cher] raising both hands out, as if one were holding the world.

reaction to complete murkiness, an impalpable 3D movie screen was projected within the clouds: recurrently emitted from the pyramid. Swiftly Belial appeared riding on a horse from the sky heading towards the podium. Proceeding, the 3D movie screen indicated that Belial was on the platform: the spotlight restored and podium heightened, as Belial sat on a rearing up white horse. Belial continued to speak immediately upon the horse's positioning on four hooves; while speaking, a halo impalpably emitted from the apex of the pyramid, visibly positioned behind Belial's crown.

"I am the prince of pacification. The new ordered propagative system was designed to consummate genuine equilibrium. Make no mistake; worship of my statue is not intended to revolutionize the Second Commandment of Allah our God Almighty. The Second Commandment was concentrated because my corporeal presence was vacuous. Now I am anatomically accessible, and undoubtedly you eyewitness my authentic image; therefore the statues' image lacks falsification, differentiated from the painting by Michelangelo. Like I am Lord over the Sabbath; my statue is a physical replacement for the duration of my absence from your municipal. Nevertheless, the Holy Spirit will remain omnipresent, but only will dwell contiguous to the statue established within your city. This new ordered machine was blueprinted from the beginning of existence as regards to our praiseworthy country, and I am honored to fulfill her purpose. God bless you all, from the Son of Man," Belial blasphemously states deeming himself as the Lord.

After the speech all leaders throughout the world paid obeisance to Belial as they walked by the podium. Suddenly a gunshot sounded. The crowd resonated an "aw" reaction while others caterwauled, witnessing Belial collapse, hand adhering his left eye. The Abeyance, Secret Service, and Egyptian Police pugnaciously searched their surroundings for a shooter; while one of Belial's Chief Minders†⁰² applied pressure towards Belial's eye socket. A helicopter escorted Belial to the nearest hospital. Thereupon entering the emergency room, the world news announced the death of President Belial.

Kirtana, Grandmother Jana, and the Devotees knew the inside scoop while the world mourned President Belial's death. Yeshua explained how everyone would shortly need to separate to complete their Domain within the Kingdom; distinctively specifying "When the dragon tilts the flag."

Several diurnal courses elapse allowing Columbia to properly show homage to President Belial. On that Saturday, the funeral's compass point was Washington District of Columbia; a stadium designed platform was constructed and ensconced on the west front of the Capitol.

If by chance a sinkhole swallowed the platform and surrounding area the world would lack practically every living tycoon; essentially every entrepreneur, king, idol, et cetera, occupied every seat or stood amongst the crowd below. In the first section sat soldiers from the Abeyance, the second section consisted of all leaders throughout the world, and the third section contained Belial's immediate family.

The crowd below the platform was separated into two sections: the first section implicated every celebrity currently in the spotlight from around the world, and the second section ensnared the common man.

Trumpets sounded as Belial's flag-enswathed coffin was conveyed by a horse-drawn caisson to quote unquote lie in state. Two soldiers from the Abeyance accompanied the horse and coffin while progressing down red carpet. Silence enslaved the atmosphere as everyone lamented in disbelief. To show respect, one and all on the outside of the second section touched Belial's coffin as the horse gaited beyond reach. When the horse arrived

02. [cheef-mahyn-der] top ranked presidential bodyguard; right hand man

at the end of the red carpet, Belial's coffin was hauled by the two soldiers and placed approximately two feet away from the podium, and horizontally towards the crowd below.

To begin the funeral service, the Pope haltingly proceeded to the podium from the second section to deliver the eulogy address, "The man lying amongst us was an awesome leader. A leader preordained to dictate; impervious to clone. Therefore why shall we attempt to solve the problematic?" Fire falls from the welkin as the Pope continues in a Dragon Accent, "Behold, a fallen Prime Mover, precipitating his thermal from the clouds." While pyre rains from the buttermilk sky, the flag from the coffin tilts. Startlingly Belial obliquely exits the coffin, one foot after another. "Welcome back my Lord," the Pope states as Belial approaches the Podium.

Every living soul jointly shared an indistinguishable appalling stare. Like déjà vu Belial performs the Welcoming Hands Gesture, expressing a deceiving benevolent snicker, concurrently occurring while pyre continued to supersede snowflakes. The Pope continues to speak while Belial stands to his right, "President Belial's positioning in relation to yours truly explains our alliance, a kinship consecrated since the blueprint of the New World. Worshiping of Belial's statue is not only an obligation, but it should be considered an honor. So without further hindrance I substantiate Belial, as Lord of the New World."

Belial stood before the crowd below, with an eye patch covering his disfigurement, and states, "Good-twilight my Fat Cats and Proletariats? I am appreciative of your prayers, in which I hearkened in a timely manner. If incertitude about my entitlement ever infiltrated your perception, I am confident the estimable Pope and Abettor cleared any disorientation," Belial laughs as he continues, "I succumbed and awakened, insomuch as I am the overlord of all including recuperation, no ophthalmic eclipse can obscure my visibility." Belial first states; first speaking in a fatigue manner, but ending with a Lion Accent while removing the eye patch from his eye.

"What individual dares to eyewitness the miracles I have performed and still deny me as Christ? Listen, thou-shalt-not entertain uneasiness, for I am a Lord of graciousness and I will provide a transcendent effort to effectuate your every requisite. While the surrounding crowd bows before me, those scrutinizing in television land shall be the crowds synonymous. For these are the Idols that ordinary citizens impersonate, and all Idols show reference to me. As I discourse at my own eulogy, know that nothing is inconceivable. Therefore we will travail interminably until every citizen's chip produces currency. There will be a disavowal of tax cuts. Each citizen will allowance ten percent of their revenue every financial transfer according to their grossed earnings. One dollar is equivalent to one Current Exchange (CE); therefore if an individual accumulates one million (CE) in one transfer, ten thousand (CE) is required for levy, no exceptions. Allah our God Almighty's economic system has survived as such since Eve convinced Adam to surf on a MacBook, and this is a modus operandi that we will cheerfully embrace. God bless you all, and once again thank you for your prayers."

Two Hundred Fifty Five Days: Preeminently, Yeshua shepherded Kirtana, Yana, Jock, and Ianto as they traveled to Jerusalem by means of the Almsgiver. The Advent of the Third Temple would soon come to past, as Yana contacted some of her Emmanuelan†[03] friends who were persecuted, but remained faithful in their Muslim converted ambient. Yana and her high-powered well-wishers met in a disclosed location to discuss the imminent mission; Akeelah Saleh—one of the investors involved with the Emmanuel tour program in Jerusalem—conversed with Yana to blueprint the mission.

"I know it has been a long time coming, but the moment has arrived, for the Emmanuelans who have been persecuted

03. [ih-man-yoo-uhl-uhn] of, pertaining to, believing in, or belonging to the way-of-life based on the teachings of Jesus Christ: God with us

for Christ to stand and fight for Jerusalem," Yana stated with a quote unquote I mean business smile.

"How do we attend to accomplish a mission as such without being killed? The Muslim Brotherhood is governing with full authority. Especially thanks to your president Belial," Akeelah stated, beginning the statement with a yell but ending with a bitter whisper.

"You know in the past, we would be in a professional cat-fight due to your aggression, but due to my yeshuanity, my anger will be rechanneled to the president remark. That is not my president! But let me introduce you to Belial's future replacement," Yana stated as Yeshua walked up to Akeelah.

"Kee Kee you no longer have to suffer for my sake, but for your suffering, your reward is now present. Come with us to construct the new temple," Yeshua stated looking into Akeelah's eyes.

Akeelah glanced at Yana with a smirk and quickly bowed at Yeshua's feet. "I have waited so long for this moment. I will follow you to any acreage.... Why, my Deity, has your second coming not been publicized throughout the New World?" Akeelah states with shock.

"This world does not search for me; therefore I have come like a thief in the night. Only the Serpent is trumpeted while he bears agony, falsely perceived as Lord," Yeshua states in a Many Ocean Accent. After Akeelah's encounter with Yeshua she contacts the Partners—a group of construction workers containing only saintly affiliates, sharing with them her inexplicable duologue with Christ, prescribing the mission at hand.

Three Hundred Sixty Five Days: marked the Advent of the New Temple, located in Jerusalem. During the systematization of the Temple, Yeshua shepherded on three different occasions, equalizing His divine presence amongst the other Devotees. On the next meeting, Yeshua would confirm if the

Temple was completely functional for its grand convene. Blown away by their crowning achievement due to Yeshua's impinging upon their ingenuity, Akeelah and the Partners were excited to display the new Temple before Yeshua. The Temple comprised many functions; in addition to Akeelah and the Partners, Yana, Jock, together with Ianto played an unparalleled role in its development:

Since Yana was the teacher she established a Saturday school room—in which resembled a classroom setting. The room contained an athenaeum including: the King James version of the Holy Bible translated into different languages, textbooks that only revealed the real truth about history, publications that were banded from bookstores to cover up a specific truth, and last but not least bible stories for children.

Jock—the best agriculturalist in Texas and arguably the whole world—cultivated a garden containing every vegetable and fruit imaginable. Apple trees and Orange trees grew close to a huge pond—where Jock raised a fish farm overflowing with tilapia. The farmland's stone path led back into the Temple's kitchen: where Jock's good friend from Texas exercised his culinary arts to become the Chief.

Ianto—a bank owner that drew up the blueprint of a brilliantly advanced financial system in Florida—expanded the Devotees online bank locality within the Temple. Ianto's bank system broke the codes of the World Bank created by Belial; strictly speaking, intelligibly modernizing the Devotees debit cards to coincide with the World Bank system.

Finally blessed with Yeshua's presence, He unquestionably approved of the Temple's celestial fabrication. Yeshua thereupon began to attract Emmanuelist who had been previously prosecuted, in conjunction with those who were previously afraid to convert to Emmanuelanity.†[04] Belial implemented

04. the quality of being an Emmanuelan through beliefs and practices, state of being Emmanuelan.

a deadline as to when the RFID chip must be implanted within the body temple; providing the Spirit of Truth, Yeshua, and the Devotees time to unshackle any human around the terra wishing to be an individualist—one opposing to commit adultery with the prostitute—resulting in the rejection of Belial's mark of the beast scheme.

Seven Hundred Thirty Days: latterly: the Temple was impregnated with born again singletons, blissful to become a spectator in Yeshua's somatic appearance. Immanuel-enthusiasts traveled throughout the globe sojourning in Jerusalem to bear witness, as well as local enthusiasts no longer intimidated to reveal their discretion of faith. Periodically the once intimidated enthusiasts expressed their boldness against Muslim oppressors, on many occasions leading to major altercations. Eventually Muslim authorities were contacted as regards to the altercations, shortly resulting in the start of a religious war.

Jesus Over Religions †[05]

As time elapsed, prayer evolved delivering exaltation to the true Creator of the earth. Yana symbolized importheousness,†[06] teaching American History to children and adults from a biblical frame of reference throughout the week days. Pastor Booker ministered on every Sabbath Saturday traveling from Texas, or his current location, via the Almsgiver. While the Temple's congregation continued to grow—although appreciative of Yana and Pastor Booker's teachings—enthusiasts began to beseech preachments from Yeshua. Not willing to deny any pleading soul with a celestial word—although it was not time—Yeshua graciously agreed to recognize their invocations.

---

05. [ri-lij-uh ns] a stumbling block created by the serpent, mixing lies with truth, in order to trick the masses into believing in more than one god; the idea of coexist.
06. [im-pawr-thee-uh-uhs] having an significant role in fulfilling a spiritual purpose

Pastor Booker displayed sensitivism†⁰⁷ regarding the financial situation of all enthusiast who attended the Temple; engendering himself a slave to their salvation. In result offering was temporized until the end of service as an option, concurrently expressing the importance of tithing. Unbeknownst to Pastor Booker, on the first occasion Yeshua attended Sabbath Saturday. Impressed with Pastor Booker's soul encouragement, Yeshua obsightlessly†⁰⁸ appeared amongst the crowd while offering transpired. Surprised by Yeshua's presence Pastor Booker smiled, bowing as he stepped aside in order for Yeshua speak.

"That in which would take an astronaut a thousand years to indicate, would take thy Lord one day. Therefore I, the Lord of Lords stand before thee from third heaven. The man in which has preached before you is one of my Devotees; a man in which I have handpicked to encourage the soul. Although he is human, I hold Booker in high regards, and deem him worthy of preaching in my precious Temple," Yeshua spoke in a Many Ocean Accent. After looking at the crowd, Yeshua focused His attention towards an impoverished woman at the pulpit as she bowed with money in her palm. Yeshua in His all-knowledge-ableness†⁰⁹ smiled as He asked the woman a resolved-question:

"Olivia! Why do you give your normal tides when in result you will be short mortgage?" Intensely weeping, Olivia looked Yeshua in His eyes and before she could declare a word, Yeshua smiles and politely interrupted her speech. "The lesson learned from Olivia is an example all should follow, faith that would move mountains and part seas. Olivia due to your faith, your mountain has been moved and no obstacle will stand in your way. Welcome to the kingdom." At that moment Jock pulled Ol-

07. [sen–si–tiv–iz–uhm] the doctrine involved in showing sensitivity, or sympathy towards another's hardship; displaying empathy
08. [awb–sahyt–les–lee] arriving at a place or location unnoticed; unusually appearing physically, the person that as arrived holds great prominence.
09. [awl–nol–i–juh–buhl–nes] knowledgeable of all things

ivia aside as his prophetic capabilities flourished in aftereffect of his yeshuanity. Thereafter, Jock delegated Olivia as one of his Geotic-Virtues, discerning that her hankering was to become a chief.

Yeshua continued to address the crowd as every enthusiasts stood in awe. "You are some of my most faithful and no one will trample this Holy ground without struggle. Therefore worship without restraint, and send your prayers to the Heavenly Father in peace. Love your enemies but do not be hesitant to profess your love for me, in result you will confuse the enemy who wishes you harm, and win over those who are blind to his devices," Yeshua states in a Many Oceans Dialect.

After Yeshua's appearance innumerable enthusiasts arose as He began to speak more frequently. Sequentially, an umpteen amount of faithful Muslims commenced to be ushered to Christ as months betided into One Thousand Ninety Five Diurnal Courses; and in the interchangeable days of sequence, the Emmanuelan population in Israel accumulated to eighty percent. Muslim authorities cogitated on why Muslim extremist suddenly began to convert to Emmanuelanity, leading to the recollection of reported altercations between Muslims and the new breed of Immanuel-enthusiasts. In result, the Muslim authorities decided to send a spy to pose as a new convertee†[10] in hopes of revealing the mystery in requisition.

Coincidently when the poseur reconnoitered the Temple, Yana was teaching one of her weekday classes for adults. Yana settled at the Temple's royal podium with a crown upon her intelligence.†[11] The crown included twelve stars, equally placed from left to right, and each star included the name of each Devotee:

"Teachings from the Quran have placed bondage on this land for centuries, but we have made progress in ushering Is-

---

10. [kuhn-vur-tee] a person who converts to another religion.
11. Revelation 12:1

rael to The Light. The sun: in which separates darkness from lightness, is displayed within every blessed second in our Deity's radiant presence. As our Shepherd leads, we, the blind, follow, touching His braille from every closed door. In result our kingdom will stand steadfastly supreme, knowing without a doubt that any ingress towards advancement is beneficial. Put the moon god Allah under your feet as I have done in the past and continuing until this day. I was once an educator in America teaching history that was untrue, the pain was like everlasting contractions until I was able to give birth to the word: the true history in which includes Jesus Christ—the word of God Almighty the Creator. Hallelujah I say, now I am free to deliver the truth in peace like an obstetrician, and you are now free to worship in peace," Yana spoke in her Arabic Accent, taking a drink of water as Yeshua stood up beside her. Yana smiled at Yeshua providing a small bow as she proceeded to finish her speech, "Jesus is a gift you know, so share the gift and save the lives of those who are still blind in this land. Our King is here to rule on earth. Help contribute to the Kingdom, our Kingdom with Christ before it is too late."

After Yana's speech thousands of enthusiasts were spiritually stimulated, contrived to guide more wandering individuals to Christ. The poseur per contra falsely interpreted the Good News as a declaration of war; and proclaimed Yana the agitator, pleading to the Muslim authorities that she should be considered as a threat to the Middle East and Belial's vision for world peace. With much convincing, the Muslim authorities bought into the poseur's claims and contacted Belial to inform him of the new threat.

In the meantime, the sole democracy in the Middle East supported the new Temple in Jerusalem and its purpose. After informed of Yana's teachings, Israel refused to act. In consequence, seven kingdoms declared war against Israel by orders of Belial: Mesopotamia, Rossiya, Roma, Misr, Turkiye, Persia, and

Columbia. Indescribably Belial said a prayer as he pronounced war against Israel for the world to hearken:

"I regret to promulgate that the perseverance for world armistice has been adjourned; due to newfangled discoveries of terrorism facing our Muslim Brotherhood. I have prayed dawn-to-dark and dark-to-dawn. Now I send an invitation encouraging all to pray to the Heavenly Father Allah our God Almighty, considering that we are unknowledgeable of our enemy's weaponry. 'Heavenly Father in the third heavens, we repent for any deficiency known and unknown. Please shepherd us in our engagement against evil. Our intendment is for world unification, but our enemy encourages war. We have attempted to love our adversaries but hostility is inevitable. I have faith that if victorious, our subjugation was only successful through you. In your moniker we pray, Amen.' It has been brought to my cognizance that the antagonist leading to the cause of our future disharmony is a former Chicago teacher, christened as Yana Obi. Yana Obi is now brainwashing the Israelis of Jerusalem to contest our Muslim Brotherhood, and the Israel military is supporting her terroristic efforts. In repercussion we have no choice but to declare war against Israel, the Middle East's sole democracy."

Yeshua was informed by the Spirit of Truth that Yana was apprehended by Muslim authorities as Belial declared war against Israel. Several altercations transpired in which lead to Yana's rescue from persecution. On one occasion, Yana was lifted off of the prison yard by one of Yeshua's Seraph and taken into the wilderness. On the second occasion, Belial attempted to drown Yana in a sea within the wilderness, but amazingly, the water was swallowed by the sea bed like an ounce of Adam's ale.†[12]

While Belial's efforts to imprison Yana failed, there was a battle in the second heaven,†[13] and lo, Archangel Michael, with

12. Revelation 12:14-16
13. Revelation 12:7-12

the stalwartness to skirmish the great dragon, compassed by his angels: compassed the great dragon and his fallen angels. Moot the New-Age Gergesenes:†[14] A nation that represents the great dragon, there is where him and his fallen angels will be casted, exemplified by thousands among thousands of dead healthy pigs, floating in Shanghai's Huangpu river; and whereas China's news headlines read Mystery of the Dead Porkers, it is revealed that the great dragon and his angels were casted to the earth, and their place would not be found any more in heaven.†[15]

Before the great dragon was casted to the earth he could be found in the second heaven, ordering his fallen angels to tempt the humans of earth, using freewill as a weapon, saying, "Come and lie with this woman, she is in you interested, and physically more interesting than your wife." Or "Come and admire this gun, embrace it to your head, liberate the trigger, and liberate your worries." Or "Lay with mankind as with womankind, if today Jesus walked the earth, this He would allow; He is the author of love, so why not love who you chose to love" Or "Jesus is not the only way to heaven, there were many religions before and after Jesus, besides the letter J was not created until after He walked the earth." Or "Live your life according to the next Or, or the Or aforementioned, why live with rules, you only have one life to enjoy," quotes fallen angel after fallen angel, and after a fallen angel is successful they report their success to the great dragon, who in return accuses the brethren of the sin before God, day in and day out.†[16]

However Yana released her contractions, birthing the Word in order to save many who were snared by an influential stumbling block, overcoming the great dragon by the blood of the Lamb, and by the word of their testimony, and they loved not their lives unto the death: for the world experienced a fall-

---

14. Matthew 8:28-32
15. Revelation 12:7-9
16. Revelation 12:10

ing away, a falling away due to the great dragon and his angel's influence, a falling away unpleasant in the eyes of Emmanuelists.†[17]

<u>One Thousand Two Hundred and Sixty Days</u> approached. Wings of a great eagle, was imprinted within Belial's memory from an encounter with Yeshua at the Downtown Islamic Center in Chicago Illinois, realizing that the wings described in Yana's first escape revealed some resemblance. On a second occasion, the feeling of dysfunction captured Belial's introspection; recollecting the supernatural event demonstrated by Yeshua. Presently rattled in his inability to tyrannize Yana, Belial was determined to devour any born again Israeli birthed from her teachings.†[18]

---

17. Revelation 12:11
18. Revelation 12:17

Clause 3
The Beasts and the Abeyance

Ere One Thousand Two Hundred and Sixty Days

Secret head, secret neck, secret shoulders, secret chest, secret thighs, secret arms, secret hands, secret legs, and secret feet: the New World's anatomy consists of all these, but without a secret groin the Prostitute†[01] and Whore†[02] would not be complete. Belial's administration exists of the Sea Beast interlocked with the Earth Beast; working collectively through secret organizations towards the union of all earthly nations. The beasts interlocking can be identified by the likeness of their lands constructed structures, and all are secrets revealed; as the Great Prostitute leaves her boot and settles in Big Apple's sea.

How art thou fallen from heaven, O Lucifer, son of the morning! how art thou cut down to the ground, which didst weaken the nations! For thou hast said in thine heart, I will sit also upon the mount of the congregation, in the sides of the north: I will ascend above the heights of the clouds: I will be like the most High:†[03] and as so the Serpent, in the eyes of infernatist,†[04] made himself like the most High, blasphemously claiming the Lord's highest praise Alleluia as one of his own aliases, Allah: the god of the fastest growing religion in the

01. Revelation 18:1-18
02. Revelation 17:12-18
03. Isaiah 14:12-14
04. a person who advertently or inadvertently believes in the Serpent as their god: by rejecting Jesus Christ, the Creator of existence, as their Lord and Savior.

New World; god nearest and dearest to Belial's heart.

<u>One Thousand Two Hundred and Sixty Days</u>: prophetically: Sinkholes open across the world as Belial inveigles Earth to a conversation, desiring to be the king of the earth, inadvertently becoming king of the bottomless pit. Enchanted by the wrath of the Prostitute's fornication, Belial extravagantly boasted about his inauguration and eulogy speech. In the after-effect coalesced with Belial's charm and charismatic character, many of the populace was deceived into believing his claim of being the Lord. The media also influenced Belial's ridiculous accusations by symbolizing him a God on magazines, and frivolously calling him Lord Belial on television.

Belial did not cease at verbal blasphemies claiming to be the Lord, but he also played God by maintaining a carnage list. FEMA camps similar to Guantanamo Bay were also maintained in the New World and preserved under the radar, specifically designed for the individuals who were on the "Most Likely to Create a Belligerent Act" list (MLCBA). The MLCBA is a list consisting of individuals who exercised freedom of speech to inform the masses about unconstitutional government proceedings; labeling the informants home terrorist within Columbia. Eventually the MLCBA evolved into an executive order entitled the National Defense Authorization Act (NDAA).

If residency was not available at FEMA camps the street became another option, as "Lord Belial's" bailout for banking companies forsakes the faithful tax payer. From the bailout, banks recovered all moneys due from their loans but nonetheless continued to foreclose their clients' homes—collecting more revenue from a sold foreclosed residence, or continued to charge high interest rates for the money owed to those struggling to stand and could not swim in a tsunami-debt home loan. As mega banks became richer—the banks responsible for the financial collapse, the middle class becomes impoverished into lower class: however as a cover up one could hear Belial deliver a resembling quote, "Let's raise the taxes on the wealthy in order to avoid a tax increase on the middle class and lower class," with the intentions of agreeing upon a conflicting result, a result interchangeable with the bailout.

Becoming a dictator in the most powerful nation in the world requires confidential sacrifices. Invitations to perform uncanny rituals at locations like Bohemian Grove revealed one's status in relation to the Prostitute. The Great Owl of Bohemia stands as the voice of the old serpent speaks from within, and instructs some of the world's most powerful leaders to perform his full-scale aspiration: ultimately for the serpent to develop the last attempt to infernate†[05] Jehovah-images,†[06] paralleling the serpent's promise to in return bestow upon Columbia controlling power over the world.

Previously releasing the Great Dragon that old serpent from the bottomless pit to embody Belial, a Bohemian Grove type ceremony also releases an antecedent king from the bottomless pit, a pope made king by the Lateran Treaty of nineteen twenty nine. Referencing Revelation Seventeen:Ten, the seventh king has continued his short space; therefore the antecedent king has embodied the pope of perdition nom de guerre the false prophet nom de guerre Earth Beast, and the time is near for Earth Beast to speak at Sea Beast's entombment.

Two Hundred Fifty Five Days: Hourglasses fill as Columbia gains more power, and the serpent slowly convinces Columbia to embrace Church vs. State in every process of law creation. In spite of Belial's claim of being the Lord, he thoroughly supported the idea of Church vs. State, inexplicably enforcing his tax levies that derived from the economic system of "Allah God Almighty." Approximately a million laws created—many in which were ridiculous—equaled one's inability to

---

05. [in-fur-neyt] to become a part of hell, in result of being sent to; and or on the path leading to hell by the influence of another.
06. [ji-hoh-vuh-im-ij] a human; made in His image - rev. Genesis 1:27

breathe without becoming a felon; mercifully Yeshua appointed two Devotees that would tag team and finally create unbiased justice, concurrently restoring any existing justice formulated from God Almighty's commandments.

Shawn Dacso and Joana Villa wrestled with Belial's Incubus in Authority visceral the judicial system's body as unjustness spread throughout the prison system, toxically spilling into the court system. With Yeshua's guidance, Shawn and Judge Villa coupled as one to single handedly restructure Canon Law, and every court proceeding apply it endogenously. Shawn, supported by God's kingdom, only handled cases pro bono, eagerly fighting against the raising prison estimate—directly caused by the Corrections Corporation of Columbia's (CCA) requirements to uphold a ninety percent prison rate. "Coincidently" however unnoticeably, Shawn fought all of his cases before Judge Villa, providing hope to the impoverished.

Visiting many prisons, Shawn learned about different program's dedicated to promulgating cases that the defendants may have been innocent but proven guilty. Endowed with discernment through the Spirit of Truth while Yeshua was aboard, Shawn was lead to the cases in which the defendants were innocent, but did not receive a fair trial due to finances. While walking through a prison overspread with kvetching offenders, Shawn traipses past a man ensconced in silence, as the Spirit of Truth corducted†[07] Shawn into the man's compass.

"Why didn't you profess your innocence as I walked pass your cell?" Shawn asked after back tracking, smirking as he swiftly engaged into a conversation.

"The question is why should I know who you are? Yes, I hear my neighbors plead their uprightness as you walk by, but they will cry to anyone who will listen. I will not waist my breath a minute longer proclaiming my innocence. In doing so,

---

07. [kor-duhkt] to pull on one's heart, usually to lead one to the truth

I would just sound crazy like the rest of these hoodlums who are clearly guilty," the man lackadaisically responds, with a chip on his shoulder.

Shawn politely gains his composure and casually looks in the man's cell, searching for an approach to continue the conversation. Anon, Shawn looks at a bookshelf in the cell and continues, "I see you have a bible, so I will assume you are a believer.

If you are innocent why have you lost the faith needed to go free?"

"It is easy for you to ask that question as a free man. I have been praying night and day for four years. Going through lawyers like water at a car cleanse. I see your bible too, so if you are a preacher, don't come to me with your judgments. I kept my faith through this whole ordeal but it has gotten me nowhere," the man states, finishing his statement as he looked out the cell's window.

Shawn reaches in to touch the man's shoulder and states, "What if I told you that your faith has paid off?"

The man turns around and glooms in Shawn's direction, looking into his eyes, "How is that when I'm still locked up in this cage?"

Smiling while continuing to hold the man's shoulder Shawn replies, "What if I told you that due to your faith, your break through has come?"

"Then I would tell you I'm listening, whether than finding your shoulder gesture offensive," the prisoner states with straightforwardness but yet with slight humor.

Shawn laughs removing his hand, "What is your name?"

"I'm Manny Sims, What about yourself?" asked the prisoner.

"You really don't know who I am, do you?" Shawn says with a snicker.

"Yes I know who you are. Shawn Dacso that hotshot lawyer from New York. Word is you were on the street homeless after you ditched that case involving President Belial. So how can you afford to fight my case? I don't have any money for you," Manny states.

Continuing to laugh Shawn states, "Let's just say that I have been blessed, and I was told to pass the blessing along to you."

After the conversation with Manny Sims, Shawn went on his way to fight Sims case. While heading to gather information for the case, Shawn was gridlocked by a group of protestors holding signs that stated, "Vote against Amendment One." One of the protestors proceeded to Shawn's vehicle requesting his support for the petition. Immediately lead by the Spirit of Truth, Shawn responded to her request.

"Do you know what this bill consist of in its entirety, or do you only wish to establish gay rights?" Shawn asked the woman with an inquiring yet puzzled expression.

"I do wish to establish gay rights we are people just like the next person. I recognized you from TV and I thought you fought for justice, but by your disposition I guess I was wrong," the female protestor stated with a disappointed demeanor.

"Yes, I have my own option on the Sapphic lifestyle, but that conversation would deter you from the truth. I know you have a phone, Google the First Amendment and you will discover what you are truly voting against. This is the question, are you willing to sacrifice your freedom to support a lifestyle?" The woman looked at Shawn with big eyes as he continued, "Follow Christ, He will not leave you blind." The woman distanced herself from Shawn's vehicle and sat on a nearby bench leaving the protestors behind; staring at her phone with a baffled stare.

Afterwards Shawn proceeded to represent Manny as Judge Villa presided. Only after two weeks of withstanding prosecutors, Manny Sims was found not guilty. Following the

Sims case, Shawn ran circles around twenty similar cases, and became known as angel judiciousness. Twenty cases multiplied into fifty as corruption became discombobulated with justice; rubbing the CCA the wrong way because of the dropping prison rate.

While walking to his car, Shawn stumbled across a woman and her family who lost their home to the foreclosure bailout. Familiar with homelessness and curious in relation to her circumstance, the Spirit corducted Shawn once again, and he was inclined to exchange discourse with the woman.

"Excuse me, I clumsily apologize," Shawn states as he trips over the woman's foot.

"You are just fine honey; it is actually my fault that I am laying on the ground for you to trip over me," the woman replied, with an expectant spirit of confidence.

"Wholeheartedly I distinguish that through no fault of your own have I tripped over you, and I hold a word placed into my mouth by the Holy Spirit especially for you: this land is not the property of a bank or a government, it is the land of your Heavenly Father, and soon He will give it back to its rightful owner," Shawn states. "Nevertheless I have a couple of friends that can help you off of the street temporarily," Concluded Shawn, handing out an Olive Street Team business card, as the woman's faith purchases a temporary abode until Yeshua's inauguration.

Judge Villa extended her arm in order to tag Shawn's hand, jumping into the ring contributing to justice. Due to celestial favor, Villa was elected a Judge in the Supreme Court, and like Déjà Vu, Judge Villa "coincidently" presided over most of Belial's NDAA cases. On a preterit date, Belial could have manipulated the cases to go in his favor using eminence. However Judge Villa impartially judged Belial's cases, using her charm to thwart any discontent created from her rulings.

Hypnotized by his attraction to Judge Villa, members from the Abeyance informed Belial of Judge Villa's influence on his process of theorization; evaluating Judge Villa's acquittals of the NDAA cases with an unclouded mind, some soldiers from the Abeyance wended to illuminate Belial on how they suspected that she was channeled by an opposing force. In essence, the soldiers reminded Belial of the essentialness to maintain control by becoming triumphal over the NDAA cases.

Inefficacious to overrule Judge Villa's rulings, Belial issued an executive order overriding the Supreme Court, enabling the Belial administration to solely control NDAA issues. Ultimately, control over the NDAA cases eliminated the First Amendment; initially attempted through the "Vote against Amendment One" movement.

From the moment that the First Amendment was invalidated: YouTube videos speaking against government decisions were immediately withloaded;†⁰⁸ any Compact Disc containing information that spoke against the government was removed from the selves; books were dislodged from the selves, and many cases burned if the contents included government bashing; radio shows airing eye-opening segments were removed from AM and PM radio waves; television programs were shut down or warned not to participate in government "affronting." From the moment that the First Amendment was invalidated, all forms of entertainment listed above were considered terrorism, and individuals associated with releasing any of these "dossiers" were subject to be placed on the MLCBA list, enforced by the NDAA.

Chivalrous protestors were greeted by Martial Law following inhuman struggles. Therefore revolutionists were less willing to contribute to marches against unconstitutional laws. Inconsiderably, religious groups took a stand with the faith that

---

08 [with-lohd] to remove from the internet due to government restrictions, or due to restrictions established by the site holder.

Jehovah-Sabaoth†[09] would provide protection. "Coincidently" throughout the protest, supernatural events puzzled soldiers of the Abeyance as they distributed Martial Law, thereupon heightening the religious groups' faith and protest voluminously. The Abeyance was stupefied when realizing aggressive struggles would not calm the protestors; labeling the immovable religious groups terrorist.

Freewill was considered void as well, completely due to the immovable religious groups. The Belial administration forced everyone to worship the Moon and Sun God—"Allah God Almighty." Eventually the Holy Bible was updated by transferring Sura from the Quran. Mandatory prayer was established for a specific time at cockcrow for the purpose of bringing order to each day, and strange chants were created to bring honor to Belial. Any refusal to adapt to the required religion was considered a form of terrorism, claiming that all other religions promoted violence. From the moment that the First Amendment was invalidated, the New World was at the mercy of Belial and the Abeyance.

Supremacy was an order, and by reason of the First Amendment's elimination, Belial's "supremacy" established no impediments; wherefore all forms of terrorism shortly became intolerable and punishable by death. Individuals placed on the MLCBA list were extirpated by drones—possibly the planes that will be used to create fire during Belial's Eulogy speech—or like normal sent to a FEMA camp within their state. While Belial spoke jocularly about drones on television, Americans with "big mouths" were silenced: violently through death or via threats by surveillance when processed with RFID chips at the FEMA camps.

Yeshua and Kirtana visited every FEMA camp throughout Columbia to spread the gospel; delivering the good news among Emmanuelan's who began to lose faith due to the cruelty executed within the FEMA camps.

"Do not be troubled and fear not, for I am here to gather my Saints for a meeting in heaven. I realize that most of you are only here due to your faithfulness towards me, thereupon those of you who die because of your faith in me will rise first, and those who Belial did not find because of their inability to bear this punishment, will rise afterwards. There, in heaven, we will prepare for battle against all who have come against thee. For this is Satan's last attempt to maul God's children, but revenge is mine and vengeance will come soon," Yeshua spoke to every camp when the torture seemed unbearable, delivering the message in a Many Ocean's Dialect yet slight Thundering Accent.

After Yeshua left each FEMA camp He revamped the heart of at least one soldier from the Abeyance within each camp. The culled soldier(s) was or were required to enlighten all Emmanuelans marked with an X of the Good News. In return the soldier(s) would avoid the wrath of Yeshua's doubled edged tongue.

The forces of justice and corruption quarreled from pillar to post as Yeshua's kingdom and the Belial administration battled for the presidency. On post, Belial encouraged abortion as taxpayers money contributed to Planned Parenthood facilities, totaling approximately five hundred million dollars each year of his legislature. A contrivance—in which was claimed to be false, but verified with the Georgia Guidestones—revealed Belial's proposal to kill ninety percent of the world's population, coinciding with the FEMA camps' assassinations. Eventually most members of Body Politic became aware of the immolations to Satan at the FEMA camps, and began to question whether God really existed.

On pillar, Yeshua stressed peaceful movements reemphasizing the fact that vengeance is the Lord's, relieving the culled soldiers of their duties, and speaking more often at the FEMA camps to inform believers about the coming events headed towards a Kingdom of Justice. While walking through one of the camps Yeshua was stopped by a man that recognized who perambulated before him, and the man confronted Yeshua with his concern.

"I know who you are good sir, as I bow at your feet with honor and relieved joy. With that being said, Emmanuelans are being killed as we speak in the next room. How can God sit back and watch something like this happen?" the man stated with a look of great concern and confusion. Yeshua looked into the eyes of every soul surrounding the man, first confronting him.

"Lucas, I do not know you but I know your father, who has prayed for you to seek my face. Therefore I mercifully say to you: Satan, who is the god of this world, has blinded the minds of those who do not believe. They are unable to see the glorious light of the Good News. When Satan was casted down from the third heaven he gained control over the earth and the heaven above earth. Life is a test of faithfulness, even I was tested by Satan and I allowed him to crucify me—so that you could have life through me, the Son of man; you will be tested alike. It is only through the Fathers mercy that you breathe from night to day, because the wages of sin is death. Can you say that you have not sinned? When I was on the cross I asked the Father 'why did He forsake me'. Now that you see me before thee with the keys of hell, you see that I am alive and well. So Lucas, I warn you; come to the Light, for I will not be amongst you long," Yeshua spoke with a Slight Thundering and Many Oceans Dialect, visibly marked with an X on His left hand and a Y on the right.

Lucas among many others—who were among the atheist—pleaded with the soldiers to be placed on the left side of the camp; as shots sounded, one of the men who remained on the right section, still blinded, replied, "Fools," shaking his head with a facial expression of disgust. After the atheist indirectly expressed his credence, he proceeded to join the other atheist: consisting of scientist and intellectuals who obtained various doctoral degrees, later becoming teachers of other individuals in some way shape or form. The irreligionists begin to dissertate on how the Holy Bible was written by humans, additionally including "scientific facts" proving why God did not exist. Moreover others discredited the Holy Bible, claiming that it was edited, altered, revised, corrupted, and/or tampered with by past generations.

Notwithstanding Yeshua's presence the "intellects" lacked commonsense, not convinced that the Man standing before them was the Son of God. Due to the intellects denial of Christ, Yeshua—a Gentleman of freewill—advanced to the left section of the camp. While the soldiers prepared to bury the deceased Emmanuelans, Yeshua rejuvenated their wounds to the point of revival before the soldiers returned. Upon returning Jehovah-Nissi confused the minds of the soldiers: not remembering the first assassination and mistaken the left section for the right. Without thinking twice the disoriented soldiers advanced to shoot the atheists, while the revived Emmanuelans auscultated through their spiritual and physical tympanic membrane from the left section of the FEMA camp.

"Pow Pow" uncontrollably stuttered Akdal Ghost as the atheists descended to the cement. Every atheist voice was distinctive, and heard on every instant that Akdal Ghost addressed the group. Thereafter the perishing of each atheist, for a second time, soldiers from the Abeyance advanced to prepare the coffins; more profoundly disoriented noticing that the coffins were prepared aforetime. Suddenly voices from the spirit world were divulged across the FEMA camp for the Abeyance and the revived Emmanuelist to distinguish.

"Lord Jesus Christ my scientific discoveries once blinded me, now that I have twenty/twenty vision, please rescue me from this place. I now believe," wailed one individual with a familiar voice; previously screaming for mercy from Akdal Ghost, and presently pleading his case after descrying Yeshua in the smokiness.

A second familiar squeal ensued after hysterically screaming for mercy from Akdal Ghost, "How stupid of me to study
books from human authors, but ignore the book written by their
Creator. How stupid, how stupid, please sweet Jesus, rescue me.
I repent, I repent," immediately nexus to another familiar cry
for mercy.

"What a fool I am for not following you all into the left
section of the camp, now that I see you all and Jesus from above,
I admit, I was the fool. Please Jesus, show mercy! Now I have
twenty/twenty vision without a series of chemical reactions
and light striking a retina. You are the only Light that I have
seen and I am in fact without a retina. I was wrong I confess,
please help. Please Lord I repent," the regretful voice shrilled
with affliction. Utterance heard from every other atheist present
during the Akdal Ghost speech eventuated laments for mercy.

While the familiar voices pleaded for mercy, the soldiers
and Emmanuelists witnessed formal sheep of the scientists and
professors torture them, repeatedly stating, "You're the reason
I'm a fiend. You're the reason I'm a fiend."

When contemplating voices and visions from the earth's
core, the Emmanuelists experienced a feeling of praiseworthy
comfort admixed with sorrow, while the soldiers underwent
comfort's antagonist. However, both parties began to bow at Yeshua's feet, and the sound of burning physique drew further, as
Yeshua closed the gate of the spirit world, responding "It is too
late," with a weeping Many Oceans Dialect.

The reverie of reality resulted in the resigning of every soldier present at the FEMA camp and brought about an
intransigent faith to the family members of the once deceased
Emmanuelists. In addition the revived Emmanuelists, many of
their family members became a part of the Olive Street Team,
committed to spreading the Good News of Gods advent Kingdom.

On Post, the Belial administration threatened represen-tatives of the Judicial Branch with indefinite unemployment: Judges, lawyers—especially public offenders, and law enforce-ment was forced to machinate the law/constitution to comply with the Georgia Guidestones and the CCA's requirements to uphold a ninety percent prison rate. Persevering on pillar, Yana continued to rule with lawfulness while other Judges were in-veigled to subterfuge the law. Belial overpassed his attraction towards Judge Yana and attempted to have her impeached. First Chronicles Sixteen:Twenty-One through Twenty-Two†[10] was the by-product of Belial's plans to attack Yana, as dysfunction captured his introspection. One extensive night, several dis-turbing dreams containing supernatural events coerced Belial's desire away from impeaching Judge Yana. When Belial gained consciousness he contacted the Pope in order for him to inter-pret the dreams.

After hours of yogism, the Pope responded to Belial's re-quest. "I have been informed by the god in which we trust; that the man in which you have had many unexplainable encounters is Yeshua, The real King of Kings, Prince of peace, Son of God Himself. We must visit Bohemian Grove in order for the Great Owl of Bohemia to put an end to my doubts, and provide the Owl with a great sacrifice," the Pope stated, interpreting Beli-al's monsacred†[11] dreams.

In desperate need of a sacrifice, Belial aspired to plan the assassination of a formal president who decided to correct his iniquities from the past. Concerned that the president would reveal government secrets due to his desire for change, Belial deemed the formal president the perfect sacrifice. The Pope and Belial came into agreement regarding the selection of the sac-rifice. Thereafter, Belial ordered soldiers from the Abeyance to

---

10. He suffered no man to do them wrong: yea, he reproved kings for their sakes, Saying, touch not mine anointed, and do my prophets no harm.
11. [mon-sey-krid] a vision from God given while asleep as a warning or insight.

shanghai the presidential sacrifice while he vacationed on his yacht. Subsequently the soldiers were to escort the formal president to Bohemian Grove.

Posterior to riding down the streets of Monte Rio California via Tactical Vehicles, the soldiers conveying the formal president finally reached their destination at nightfall. Pyre revealed the Owl of Bohemia at sundown, while the Pope and Belial gathered with others preparing for the great sacrifice. Suddenly the Prince of Darkness spoke after the required amount of Satanism transpired.

"Fools haven't you learned? God does not hear your puny prayers. You are not worthy to be in His presence and in no position for Him to hear your request. You are like me. Ha Ha Ha, fools, fools. This man you present to me is a buffoon-awful case. I attempted to teach him when he held office, but he was worthless, worthless! Now Belial, you attempt to pray to God for guidance with a war against Israel, you are the biggest fool of them all. You are fighting a war against God. It is true, your struggles have been against Yeshua, and like the weak human that you are He has overpowered you. Fool, but I will forgive you on one occasion; execute this president that you provided as a sacrifice before me. In result you will send a message to past presidents, proving that you are truly the Kings of Kings, the One; with executive power to demand respect," the Prince of Darkness spoke in a Lions Dragon Accent. Shots fired as the formal president fell to his death forthwith.

Following the satanic ceremony Belial and the Pope headed into the encampment, where all members proceeded to comment fornication with high profile prostitutes. While the Executive Powers enjoyed their festivities, soldiers from the Abeyance took the president back to his yacht, in order to stage a murder.

At day peep, the media reported the formal president's death a homicide, as the world awaited for an explanation in the process of investigation. When the New World paid homage to the president, all leaders throughout the terrene attended. The Pope and Belial spoke as two of the guest speakers; extending their condolences to the president's family. Belial ended his speech by blaming the terrible tragedy on home terrorism, and pledged to enforce gun control due to the unsolved murder investigation.

Soldiers from the Abeyance preformed drumrolls as they marched to establish marital law throughout every neighborhood. Belial rigorously dictated his powers to enforce executive orders, thereupon assembling the New World into a dictatorship: following the orders of the Prince of Darkness. The Abeyance performed mandatory searches for any firearms and ammunition within each domicile. Any hindrance resulted in Resisting Pursuit, an offense punishable for up to thirty days in prison. Eventually any individual in possession of a firearm was considered a home terrorist, an offense punishable by death.

<u>Nine Hundred Thirty Days</u>: marked the posthaste approaching event that Emmanuelans have called the Rapture, and many Hollywood movies have denominated alien evasions. Belial and Yeshua continued to rhubarb from pillar to post as the worldist†[12] assumed that the god in which Columbia trusted would continue to reign over Yeshua's Kingdom.

On post, the Pope encouraged the masses to evolve into the process of worshiping Belial's statue. Lack of prayer was considered the cause of the rapidly diminishing world economy. Therefore every individual was required to worship the Belial statue within their town; reiterating that the statue was the only place that the Holy Spirit would dwell. A well-known Emmanuelan leader began to rebel against the worship of Belial's statue, convincing many believers and nonbelievers to follow his lead:

"My people do not be deceived. Jehovah is the only controller of the Holy Spirit, so who is the Pope to say otherwise?

12. [wurl-dist] to remove from the internet due to government restrictions, or due to restrictions established by the site holder

We must fight. We have been peaceful Emmanuelans centuries too long. We must protect our rights at all means, and we must not lie down while we are trampled on. I will not worship Belial's statue. I will only worship Jehovah, and I will end my prayers in Jesus name, the real King of kings may I add, not a president that yearns to become God. I will not compromise, and to you my beautiful brothers and sisters; I would forewarn you to do the same. I know that some of you look at me as a kibitzer, but my advice stems from love. Now repeat after me 'stand up no we won't', and rise up against Belial's dictatorship. Come on repeat after me. 'Stand up! No we can't! Stand up! No we won't! Stand up! No we can't! Stand up! No we won't!'" the Emmanuelan extremist screams as his followers rant alike, failing to consult with God before his revolutionist act, and protesting near a Belial statue while others worshiped. Suddenly limitless drones invaded the atmosphere with bombardment, killing the protestors for the worshipers of Belial's statue and the tentative to attest.

Socialism contributed to Belial's aspiration to acquire predomination over humanity, as healthcare slowly became a monopoly controlled by the government. After the Supreme Court passed the proposed act regarding the usurpation of healthcare, the ground was set for the Belial administration to plan the installing of the implantable National Medical Device Registry—Also known as the RFID chip—in every citizen throughout the New World. The masses were swindled into believing that the proposed healthcare act was formulated to benevolently provide healthcare to those in necessitation, unaware of the contents within the one thousand page bill. On page: One Thousand One—section: Two Thousand Five Hundred Twenty-One, the mark of the beast shifty revealed itself, hidden in plain sight by Belial's use of political nomenclature interfusion. Any refusal to acquire Belial's healthcare would require an additional tax reduction, garnishing a large percentage from each certificate of indebtedness; any further refusal would eventually result to the inability to buy or sell.

Like those who refused Belial's health bill, the world's economy shared similar interest refusing to uphold; therefore as opposite attracted, eventually married immediately, and those who refused Belial's Mark inadvertently refused to buy or sell. Resultantly, the plan to implant the implantable emanated. The United Nations organized an assembly including every leader throughout the world to "institute a solution" in order to maintain order, and stay afloat in a world drowning in debit. Belial was safeguarded to the United Nations Headquarters via The Beast—the moniker of Belial's vehicle—for the meeting to revive the world's economy, and Belial was deemed the savior against the evil Collapse Economy.

"The following assembly is impenetrable to any source of announcement; any person(s) entangled in the discharge of the information revealed within this engagement will meet disestablishment. As we were informed, the economy of the world has disintegrated, therefore order must be maintained. I have the necessary executive orders implemented to indubitably predicate normality. If any member of law enforcement forbears to perform the necessary propositions to maintain normality their employment will be revoked, and any compliant member of law enforcement will be a coconspirator under a member of the Abeyance. With that being communicated, the dollar bill is abandoned, and the love of the dollar bill is consistent within the vascular organ of most humans. Ergo most individuals will welcome the installment of the Radio-frequency identifier, considering that it will be the solitary source of income, and the reconstruction of the dollar bill. The Radio-frequency identifier is conjointly a Global Positioning System and body mike; therefore the movements of every human will be revealed eliminating crime. If by chance the populace rejects the original implementation, the nations may be forced to methodize World War Three in order to further impair the economy, and heighten compulsion towards a steadfast governing of the BoP.†[13] Welcome to the New World my statuesque colleagues, by courtesy of the Vatican—leaders of the Pyramid—underneath the God in which we trust; we are now the Kings of the universe," Belial addressed the crowd in a Lions Accent, as his mixed complexion favored a leopard.

The leaders of each nation traveled aboard, and into their own countries to spread the fabricated solution directed toward performing CPR on the Titanic economy; while Belial proceeded to familiarize Columbians of the implementations "agreed upon" between every nation on the terrene. Indirectly the New World deemed Belial the President of Sphere Earth, claiming that no other nation could make war against Columbia. Therefore technically, the Pope directly deemed Belial the President of the New World by first manipulating Belial's birth certificate, making Columbia's State Out Of the Sea his new birthplace. Just as the Radio-frequency identifier was "publicly agreed upon," each leader addressed their endemic nation of the New Order.

JESUS Over Mammon

The main event included the Pope and Belial standing parallel, as the Beasts addressed Columbia, "My Emmanuelans! It is written, a mark will be received in the right hand or the forehead, and to avoid actions such as these. However, Revelation is a chapter full of metaphors and should not be taken literally. There is no such creation as a dragon, and there is no animal that has the appearance of a leopard and the feet of a bear. Our God is more intelligent than any human that ever walked

---

13. [bee-oh-pee] the bottom of the pyramid

the earth. Therefore why would He create a creature with seven heads, ten horns, and place the crowns on the horns not the head? Thence, I say to you, as Holy Father of earth, the Mark of the Beast is not a microchip that one will implant in their bodies, that is a myth originating from the garbage polluting the internet. I only wish you blessings, and I would not attempt to play a part in the condemning of your soul.

The Radio-frequency identifier is an instrument that will contain your medical records, thus in case of an unexpected emergency the paramedics can provide the best care possible catering to your unique medical condition. Terrorism is at an all-time high, clearly displayed with the murder of your formal President, and also displayed in the attempted murder of our president, King and Lord, Belial. Identity thief is also at an all-time high in relation to terrorism, as terrorist will maintain continuous efforts to murder innocent bystander's partaking in pseudo-identity.†¹⁴ Hence only for your wellbeing we expounded the Radio-frequency identifier, a solution created to eliminate any pseudo-identity as well as hold your medical records. So without further ado, Belial, Lord of the New World, will continue to provide the necessary details in order to obtain the identifier," the Pope spoke with a Dragons Accent in all of his agedness, particularizing a "dinosaur": the beast of the Mesozoic Era; as Belial in his vigorousness particularized the Lion: the beast of the New Age.

"I come before you to address the sudden crash of the world's economy. For the purposes of reaching those who are benighted and/or with mental deficiencies, I will limit the use of political wheedle to stress the importance of the times forthcoming. Just as my mentor mentioned succeeding myself, the Radio-frequency identifier formally known as the Registry, will allow the government to continue the flow of currency with

14. [soo-doh-ahy-den-ti-tee] spuriously pretending to be another person other than one's birthed being; identity thief

the elimination of the banknote. The perks of the registry will indeed include medical and personal information, as well as a stimulus currency transfer—enough for one to open a small business for the hopes of creating additional sources of employment. Unfortunately due to the elimination of the banknote, the Registry will be the only source of currency. Surgery in regards to the Registry will be financially covered under the new healthcare bill. My administration is working unendingly to create other methods to restore the world's economy. Although the Registry, if used with wisdom, will be a tool of great possibility," Belial stated, creating applause from the crowd, "Thank you," Belial ended; proceeding to a secret location in which he would mingle with members of the synagogue of secret sins; not concerned with repentance, but with the beauty of the Prostitute's fornicatory.

After Belial's address on "overcoming the condition of the economy," hospitals transfigured into pandemonium as the hoi polloi desperately scrambled to undergo RFID chip surgery in the forehead or right hand. The Secretary proceeded with each procedure only after each patient was tested and approved by four departments: the Commissioner of Food and Drugs, the Administrator of the Centers for Medicare and Medicaid Services, the head of the Office of the National Coordinator for Health Information Technology, and the Secretary of Veterans Affairs. The four departments collectively ensured that the chip contained the correct information for each patient, and that the body would not reject the chip. Implantation of the "Registry" was required between but not succeeding Thirty Six months, providing time before One Thousand Two Hundred and Sixty Days to fleetly infernate Jehovah-images.

Snared on post in behalf of socialism, Belial appropriated control over all natural resources via an executive order entitled: National Defense Resources Preparedness. The world's economy as a whole became enslaved under the executive order:

directly stating that Columbia's government would be exempt from the order nevertheless containing contractible vernacular, indirectly including Columbia's citizens, and all other nations of the world. In layman's terms, the Belial's administration and any following administration officially gained complete control over the New World: a New World created by Columbia, and a New World consisting of every nation on the globe. While the serpent fulfilled his promise to Columbia he began to realize that his time was almost up, as the calendar revealed: <u>One Thousand Two Hundred and Sixty Days</u>.

Clause 4
Separation of Church and State

Amid the year of One Thousand Six Hundred Twenty Anno Domini, the Mayflower "Saints": also known as the Pilgrims, inquired a contrivance to constitute a "New Jerusalem"; in result the entitlement New World was simulated, an agenda installed into the Pilgrims mind by the serpent: "god of this world," while the Pilgrims arrogantly assumed that they were particularly chosen by God Almighty: God of the universe. After the Mayflower settled at an unknown destination, the Pilgrims eventually proceeded to act as gods in their "New Jerusalem" and deceivingly took over the land of the Indians—the Indians who helped them adapt to their unknown destination. Succeeding, familiar with the connotations in the Holy Bible regarding the characteristics of Jesus Christ, the Mayflower "Saints" were terrified when witnessing the bronze skin[01] depicted in the description of the King of kings, displayed within a human. To further prove their dominion as gods—conquering their fears, the Pilgrims progressed to enslave the Emmanuel resembling humans, obtaining hegemony that would endure for centuries.

Forefather of the Earth Beast, Rodrigo Borgia: son Cesare Borgia, and Leonardo Da Vinci preformed blasphemies amongst one another influencing Leonardo to paint Cesare as the King of kings. The Catholic Synagogue of Satan appointed Rodrigo Borgia as Pope Alexander VI, allowing him to publicly display the painting of Cesare, evolutionally deceiving the world thereafter, leaving Lord Jesus Christ to be portrayed as corruptible.[02] The Pilgrims, thenceforth, embraced the painting of the false Christ for the purposes of keeping the enslaved Africans low spirited, simultaneously convincing the slaves that

01. Daniel 10:4-6, Revelation 1:12-16, Revelation 2:18
02. Romans 1:18-23

they were inferior to them—those in which God "particularly" chose, demanding the slaves to ergo address them as master. In addition, any slave convicted of reading would be killed; enabling slaves the resources to uncover the truth, the truth that would set the slaves free, and that truth is the biblically correct characteristics of the Son of Man/Godhead.

Centuries elapse as the New World evolved into Columbia and the laws established mostly from God Almighty's Ten Commandments characterized Columbia as a Christian nation. However as Presidents passed through the executive branch, Columbia dilatorily departed from God, successively revealing Columbia's original propose/uninterrupted sequence; inspired by the serpent. Every president that was found guilty of interrupting the original propose would be killed.

One Thousand Six Hundred Twenty Anno Domini transmuted into Eighteen Sixty Five Ann Domini, leading to the creation of the Thirteenth Amendment, officially setting slaves free in the fruition of unalterable faith that a change would come. Unfortunately, the first president found guilty of interrupting Columbia's original propose technically was responsible for the freedom of slaves, and thereafter was assassinated. The first documents involved with providing slaves their prerogatives was through an executive order called the Emancipation Proclamation, amalgamated with and finalized by the Thirteenth Amendment.

Inspiration for the executive order originated from God Almighty, as the president made it a point to include "the year of our Lord" several times within the executive order's contents. Although Columbia's original propose was inspired by the serpent, God Almighty remained in control, changing the heart of a king: the only justification leading to the misconception that Columbia ever intended to become a Christian nation.

Approximately one hundred years outdistanced Eighteen Sixty Five Ann Domini, and a new king who was of African descent emanated, a king just as influential than the kings appointed by Columbia in Eighteen Sixty Five Ann Domini and the nineteen sixties synthesized; a king dayably†[03] momentous due his Pastor entitlement, unlike Columbia/the State, a man unquestionably influenced by God Almighty. While Pastor King peacefully harmonized marches against continued injustices, there became a great conflict between: Pastor King's propose and Columbia's original propose; in result Pastor King was marked for americide.†[04]

The Civil Rights Act of Nineteen Sixty was created and signed due to a powerful Civil Rights Movement, ultimately lead by Pastor King. In opposition, Secret Society Ku Klux Klan incalculably contributed to the Prostitute's secret groin of fornication. Claiming to be Christian, the Secret Tripled K Society was also aware of the Bible's description of the Son of Man. Therefore as their trademark, crosses were burned to express their disapproval of African Americans; a trademark inspired by the serpent: who continuously enjoyed even the slightest resemblance of Lord Jesus' crucifixion.

The mission to create a New Jerusalem on earth would crumble with a New Order: an order completely separate from Jehovah; since Columbia was "christened" as the New World she intended to relinquish existence as a New World with a new order, blasphemously characterizing herself as the Alpha and Omega, the Beginning and the End.

---

03. [dey-ey-blee] worthy of naming a day after
04. [uh-mer-i-sahyd] the killing of an American that fight's against Columbia's "original propose."

Ere One Thousand Two Hun- dred and Sixty Days

<u>One Thousand Two Hundred and Sixty Days</u>: prophetically: When reelected, Belial indefinitely separated Columbia from the Emmanuelan church and only considered two options: infamously govern the church, or slowly invalidate the churches that were unsacrificeable.[05] During these troubling times Yeshua only accepted the radiant church: without stain or wrinkle or any other blemish, but holy and blameless; using out of His mouth a doubled-edged sword to make the church holy: by cleansing through The Word. Maintaining a radiant church was intensely quintessential, considering that the serpent embodied Belial to promptly invalidate the unsacrificeable church through the exposer of discreditable sinningness.

<u>Two Hundred Fifty Five Days</u>: Pastor Booker, the new aged John the disciple, traveled the world via the Largesse to deliver revelations from Yeshua; to correct any blemish within the church, for the members of the congregation emblematized the current Disciples and were the only representation of Jesus to the nonbeliever. A blameless church would be ideal to limit the amount of infernatist,[06] but unfortunately the prostitute's influence was not limited to the streets. The serpent cultivated a new boldness ambulating throughout the house of God, taking cruel measures of beguilement while humanity attempted to find salvation; with the hopes of deluding any member or

05. [uhn-sak-ruh-fahys-ey-buhl] unwilling to be put forth as a sacrifice to the serpent; reluctant to bend the truth written in the Holy Scripter for the purposes of an earthly acceptance or advancement
06. [in-fur-ney-tist] a person who is a part of hell, in result of being sent to; and or on the path leading to hell by the influence of another

follower of the congregation into spiritual homelessness.

Congregations of the New Age possessed at least one characteristic—in which they were judged by—mirroring one or more of the churches from Asia of old: Ephesus, the church at the end of the apostolic age; Smyrna, the church under persecution; Pergamos, the church of the world; Thyatira, the church influenced by the prostitute; Sardis, the church close to homelessness but slightly sheltered; Philadelphia, the church in the Light; and Laodicea, the sacrificeable†⁰⁷ church. Yeshua inspirited Pastor Booker as judgment was sermonized by the mouth of a doubled edged sword:

Holy Ephesus Ministries was a mega church with a professional environment undifferentiated from a place of business, and misrepresentation concerning the Lord Jesus Christ in any form of vileness was not tolerable. Any guest apostle operating under the tabernacle of Satan revealed through the Spirit of Truth was brazenly rebuked in private—ensuing their preachment, following an apology from Pastor Gianni addressing the members that divulged in the apostle's soulinjurious†⁰⁸ intentions. Preferentially Saint Nicholas was not entertained, avoiding the ways of the Pagan heathen: one that will cut down a tree from the forest and deck it with silver and gold.†⁰⁹

Moreover as a form of benefaction, three days out of the week—known as the Delivery days—excluding Sunday, Ephesus Ministries organized charity functions in neighborhoods that even law enforcement avoided due to safety measures. During the Delivery Days, Ephesus Ministries could be found devotedly—by means of promotional vans imprinted with Jesus crucifixions—traveling through neighborhoods of crime

---

07. [sak-ruh-fahys-ey-buhl] willing to be put forth as a sacrifice to the serpent for the purposes of financial advancement and or acceptance
08. [sohl-in-joor-ee-uhs] baleful, cruel, or damaging, as in effecting or attempting to effect the soul
09. Jeremiah 10:1–4

and poverty. Gang members of the neighborhoods remarkably avoided confrontations with the Ministry respecting their role in the community.

Even though members of the gangs avoided confrontation with Ephesus Ministries while in their neighborhoods, on several occasions the gang members followed the church members back to their prosperous environments. In result many robberies transpired. Knowing that the robbers were members of the neighborhoods in which they served did not deter the ministry from the continuance of charity events in the same communities; ultimately leading some of the gang members to Christ.

JESUS OVER GANGS

Sunday services at Holy Ephesus Ministries operated systematically characterless as Pastor Gianni displayed the same no-nonsense facial expression at every sermon, shortly emulated throughout the ministry. The atmosphere of the church resembled a business of God excluding the alternativeness of a house of God. Jehovah God has many appellations, one inheres in Jehovah-Sabaoth: the Lord of Host, Whom alone is Holy and is the definition of love; not one of His congregations is Holier than He. Therefore no congregation regardless of its wealth or development should possess a Holier than thou attitude, abandoning the most important fruit of the spirit called love.

Yeshua recollected the prayer from a single soul, a foster child whose request was to obtain parental guidance and love not provided from her foster parents; fighting the temptations of prostitution and the desire to find a boyfriend at her young age, in order experience love:

"Dear Jesus, if you are real I hope you are listening. All I want is to be loved, for someone to ask me how my day is going and hug me from time to time. I need someone to tell me that they love me once in a while. See my mother and father died when we got into a car accident, and I was the only survivor. I was a new born, or so I was told. The point is, I never got to hear them tell me that they loved me. If they did I was too young to recall. I have been thinking about selling myself, but not necessary for the money. It would just be nice for someone to look at me like I am important enough to spend money on or for. I thought about getting a boyfriend but I think I am too young for that right now. I spoke to one of friends who told me about your love, and encouraged me to attend a church. My only memory of your presence was through a church called Holy Ephesus Ministries. I remember how the church provided assistance in my neighborhood, but the lasting impression imprinted in my mind was the lack of love revealed within the ministry. They didn't smile while assisting and it was like they were just doing their job. So since they are a representation of you, I don't think that you could feel my quest for love, but I figured that it was worth a shot to ask. I wish that you could but I just don't know. I wish that I could see you also because I feel like a crazy person talking to myself. If you are up there I want to go to church and find the truth, but again it just seems like the Pastor and his associates at Ephesus Ministries are just there for the pay check, and that is the only church van that comes to my neighborhood. Well, I don't know, talk to you later, I guest, Bye.... Oh! He-he-he, by the way my name is Deshae Ieshia Jenkens."

Thousands of prayers were perceived by Yeshua showing reference to Holy Ephesus Ministries, praising God Almighty for His providence accomplished through the congregation. However the prayer from Deshae Jenkens placed a lasting impression in Yeshua's cognizance, hence He sent Pastor Booker to convey a warning to Holy Ephesus Ministries, appertaining to Candlestick Ephesus†[10]—the church at the end of the apostolic age, coincidently leaving Holy Ephesus Ministries guilty

10. Revelation 2:1

by affiliation-epithet.†[11] Yeshua inspirited Pastor Booker to sermonize from Matthew Twenty-Five:Forty-Three through Forty-Six.

"I have come on behalf of President Yeshua, the King of kings, Son of Man, Son of the Most High God; who has come like a thief in the night upon the world and a thief in the night upon the church. I am the new aged John the disciple, and by your judgment of character through the help of the Comforter, you know I tell the truth. I will sermonize from Matthew Twenty-Five:Forty-Three through Forty-Six. Let us stand for the reading of the Word," Pastor Booker begun his preachment; while the leaders and members read the Word of God, for then the voices of the mega church coalesced as one, 'I was a stranger, and ye took me not in: naked, and ye clothed me not: sick, and in prison, and ye visited me not. Then shall they also answer him, saying, Lord, when saw we thee an hungred, or athirst, or a stranger, or naked, or sick, or in prison, and did not minister unto thee? Then shall he answer them, saying, Verily I say unto you, Inasmuch as ye did it not to one of the least of these, ye did it not to me. And these shall go away into everlasting punishment: but the righteous into life eternal,' the church quoted along with Pastor Booker.

"Amen, amen," Pastor Booker stated, continuing with his preachment. "Now church I ask you: why have you clothed the naked, nurtured the hungry and thirsty, and visited those in prison to minister to them? It is because of your love for Him, thus said the Lord. Howbeit, Satan constructed a clever plan and inflicted Jesus with amnesia, causing Him to contemplate prostitution. So why did you walk by this blasphemous act and not inform the Lord of His true identity? I ask you, is that love?" Pastor Booker preaches.

Immediately the church turned to one another with con-

11. [uh-fil-ee-ey-shuhn-ep-uh-thet] conceding that the meaning of a person, place, or thing's name defines it's character

fused and tenantless stares following Pastor Booker's catechism. Suddenly a young woman walks up to the podium, in tune with the Spirit, Pastor Booker smiles and gives the woman the microphone.

"I have been living eighteen years and haven't felt love like I have here today. I was a sinner but now I give my life to Jesus Christ, because no one will love me like He will. Pastor, I am not sure of your name, and I am not familiar with Apostle John, but I know you are not a leader or member in this church. Don't get me wrong Holy Ephesus Ministries have done wonders in the community, but Pastor you are the first leader in this church that I have seen smile. Your message was not only for the church it was for me, as members and leaders looked around with confusion...." the young lady breaks down and cries, trying to catch her composer in order to finish her sentence. "This is the first time that I have learned to hear God's voice, first telling me to come to church this morning and second telling me to speak in front of an unfamiliar audience; so excuse me.

... As I was saying, while you all looked around with confusion about Jesus being tempted into prostitution, I understood that figuratively Jesus took my place. And it is a miracle that Jesus heard my prayer over probably a thousand others and delivered this message to me in order to prove His love. And for that, I hand over my life.... I love you Jesus," the woman states; after speaking, she hands Pastor Booker the microphone, runs off of the stage and out of the church doors crying with joy; while Pastor Booker closed his conveyance of a warning from Jesus:

"The young woman that just ran out of the church doors was Deshae Ieshia Jenkens, this is a young lady I have never seen, met, or know anything about. What I can tell you is that she did not feel love when encountering this ministry. A thousand prayers eulogizing your ministry in Jesus' name equals one prayer from a lost young lady searching for a love not found in your ministry. The church is the only representation of Christ to the nonbeliever, so love should be the first characteristic displayed when someone encounters your ministry. Remember, Lord Jesus loves first and corrects later. So if you are being corrected as you are now, you are fully aware of His love. Therefore REPENT, THUS SAID THE LORD, make this church like a house of God vs. a corporation of God. YOUR WORKS ARE GREAT BUT YOUR FIRST WORKS SHOULD BE LOVE. Smile as you would if the Lord was in your presence. REPENT ANON, or from this church the Lord will remove His candlestick, in which represents His Holy Spirit. God bless you all. Seek blessings!"

Seriatim to Deshae Jenken's testimony and Pastor Booker's conveyance of a warning, Kirtana accompanied as Yeshua walked up to the podium and performed a Raising Hands Gesture. Every knee of the mega church uncaringly bowed; comfortably through the perceivedness of the Average Joe's observation, but uncomfortableness was obvious to the Sagacious Personage because of the space between the aisle and the seating. Nexus of spiritual reasoning the Average Joe would represent the believer and the Sagacious Personage would represent the nonbeliever. Nevertheless all heads bowed and all knees bent because not all who attended this evening were believers, but in fact there were many Deshae Jenkens' in attendance, not knowing before, but currently witnessing the love of Jesus from Deshae Jenken's testimony and Yeshua's welcoming pierced hands. While Pastor Booker proceeded to exit the church Yeshua stated, "I love you all," and the Shepherd humbly followed His Devotee.

The approaching of <u>Four Hundred Fifty Five Days</u> lead Belial—who was overtaken by the spirit of the serpent—into a frantic state assimilating his soon to come destiny, desperately endeavoring more tweet-able followers @lake-of-fire-burning-with-brimstone before time expired. As a result Belial strictly enforced the National Defense Act, previously deeming any Church that was not corporative to his new religion a home terrorist. An unsacrificeable sanctuary called Church of Repentance was one of Belial's first targets; hence the sanctuary obtained the personality of Candlestick Smyrna.†[12]

Church of Repentance was a sanctuary of nearly no blemish in the eyes of the Lord, generally because it was in an imperfect world. Located in an undesirable area, Church of Repentance underwent many opportunities to leave the "ghetto" but choose not to transpose. No person regardless of race, creed, background, lifestyle, appearance, style of dress, et cetera, was ever rejected from the church—a church with an atmosphere equivalent to walking into grandmother's home, and "trouble makers" in specie were encouraged to attend. Last but not least, persons of low or no income were also encouraged to attend and basically made up most of the sanctuary's members.

Beneficence was not a stranger to Church of Repentance, any member or person from the street was provided charity; considering that the seed administered was not planted on bad ground. "It's alright, repent mimicking the Light" was the church's sportive motto, inspiring the self-ordealist†[13] to turn to Christ and reminding those who are born again to strive toward correction of the repentant sin or sins.

While Church of Repentance brought souls to Christ for more than ten years, God Almighty continuously created financial miracles due to the shortage in tithes. Pastor Bryant—head and founding Pastor of the church—desiderated a mega church in order to reach a wider audience, but understood his members financial situations and therefore was satisfied with God's current providence. Nevertheless certain leaders—forming Clique Apollyon—underhandedly plotted on a solution to relocate the church using unseemly resources. In order to carry out the plan, many of the members were unlawfully incarcerated and held

12. Revelation 2:8
13. [self-awr-deel-ist] a person who has convicted themselves to hell, thinking that God would not forgive their particular sin(s)

without trail under the aegis of the National Defense Act.

Pastor Bryant—unaware of the evil plot—was puzzled on how his church members were suddenly becoming incarcerated in abundance. Immediately Pastor Bryant contacted the sanctuary's lawyer and member John Johnson to have the incarcerated church member's released. Nonetheless, little by little, member by member, Church of Repentance was successively attacked by the Judicial System under an indirect order of Clique Apollyon, and under a direct order of the serpent—who wanted to exploit the church because they were highly favored by God.

Prayers from Pastor Bryant asking for deliverance regarding the attacks led Yeshua and Pastor Booker to Church of Repentance, as Yeshua inspirited Pastor Booker to sermon a conveyance of a warning. Relying on Jehovah's providence once again, Pastor Bryant knew the visitation from Pastor Booker was an answer to his prayers and allowed him to take the pulpit.

"I am Pastor Booker the new aged Apostle John. I have come on behalf of President Yeshua, the first and the last, which was dead, and is alive. Like He was crucified, died, and rose again, you will be incarcerated and have tribulation for ten days. Be faithful unto death, when you arise from the first death the Lord will give you the crowns of kings and queens, inherited into the kingdom of the most high God; avoiding the second death. There will be some leaders who will be relieved from the tribulation, in this occasion relief is not of the blessed, for the relieved are secretly members of the synagogue of Satan, and hence the second death is their fate. Pastor Bryant, don't you realize Church of Repentance is your mega church? Your poverty is of this current world, why don't you realize that you are rich? Thou iron rod lies within one thousand years of Yeshua's ruling on earth. God bless you all. Seek blessings!"

Pastor Bryant received discernment that Pastor Booker was truly the new aged Apostle John, but due to Yeshua's omniscience He apperceived that some members and leaders had doubts about Pastor Booker's identity. Thus Yeshua walked up to the pulpit forthwith, speaking with a Many Oceans Dialect, "Do not fear, I am the King of kings, Son of Man, the only Lord Jesus Christ. I have come to confirm Pastor Booker's claim to be the New Aged John, the only Pastor of my twelve Devotees. Church of Repentance, you hold the Candlestick of Smyrna. Hence Belial will throw you all in a FEMA camp in your ten days of tribulation, but know that I am with thee. Do not worry about your family I will provide shelter for them. Death is inevitable, but everlasting life is only granted through me. Therefore do not be ashamed or afraid to keep my doctrine; your loyalty will not go unrewarded. I will provide you with crowns of kings and queens, ruling with an iron rod over the nations. I love you all; you soon will not undergo pain any longer."

Yeshua and Pastor Booker exited swiftly. During Yeshua's address to the church, all those in attendance joyfully bowed. Shortly after the departure of Yeshua and Pastor Booker, the Abeyance kicked down the church doors and proceeded to arrest everyone in attendance. Gracefully Pastor Bryant, leaders, and members—due to the presence of the Holy Spirit—were handled with care and transported to the nearest FEMA camp.

Ten days of tribulation bore resemblance to Guantanamo Bay styled torture tactics. The first five days were designed with the intendment of causing doubt in the minds of the fair to middling Emmanuelist, attempting to prove that Jesus did not exist. Documentaries hybridizing Jesus with other "gods" were created in the form of videos, blasphemously using such comparisons as the following: Amen with Ra; Jesus with Horus and Krishna; the Cross with the Ankh; Jesus and Mary with Aset and Heru; God Almighty, Jesus, and the Holy Spirit with Allah, Prophet Mohammad, and the Black Stone. New Secular music was also used to cloud the mind, playing two or three songs concurrently: reaching volumes of one hundred decibels.

Diurnal courses five through ten were dedicated to falsely

expressing that if Jesus did exist He was not concerned, stressing that many Emmanuelists had previously been assassinated; passionately betokening that the rapture was folktale and Jesus would not commission disentanglement from their tribulation. With reference to Church of Repentance, most of the members and all leaders overcame the first five days, and emerged into the last five diurnal courses with a John Fourteen:Six Attitude. Per contra, physical torture in the last five days nearly broke the congregation's spirit. The survival rule of threes was used against Church of Repentance as the Abeyance refused to provide food and water; collectively becoming an inhabitant in a highly insolated environment.

After day four without comestible and aqua, waterboarding was used as a form of dualized torture:†[14] an identical question followed by the wrong answer paralleled an identical action, as "Do you believe in Jesus?" and waterboarding alternated ensuing a response of "Yes." On the eventual diurnal course, Bushmaster contributed to patronizing the Abeyance in the last endeavor to coerce the Emmanuelists into denying Jesus. Approaching midnight, the Abeyance proceeded to prepare the coffins in order to fill them with the unsacrificeable Emmanuelists: therefore Yeshua addressed His crown worthy Sheep before they faced death.

"You will soon be with me in the heaven above, so still do not fear. Your deaths will not include pain, therefore picture the weaponry as the way to the Father's everlasting kingdom. Do not hold resentment in your heart before your demise; instead pray to the Father to forgive them for their sins. In result some of your enemies will become your brothers in Christ, departed from the serpent, for those know not that they are being used. Your tribulation is now over, well done," Yeshua spoke of sovereignty in a Many Oceans Dialect, and departed as soldiers from the Abeyance prepared to ally with Bushmaster.

14. Torture maximized twofold

While the soldiers began to discharge Remington SPC's from the left section of the FEMA camp, "Lord forgive them for they know not what they do" was heard before every word that Bushmaster spoke. After every leader and member from Church of Repentance passed into royalty, many of the soldiers were inspired from Luke Twenty-Three:Thirty-Four and gave their lives to Christ: immediately followed by their demise. Many other churches equivalently suffered a ten day tribulation due to their influential opposition to the serpent, receiving the personality of Candlestick Smyrna.

The Vatican, also known as the Roman Catholic Church, also known as the Catholic Synagogue of Satan: creator of Islam: holding the doctrine of Balaam, creator of Paganism: holding the doctrine of the Nicolaitans: is not also known as the entire Catholic Church, and thou—in which are not also known as—will be giving a new name written on white stone, in order to be disassociated from their currently infamous characterization. Such disassociation would require courage and would threaten their livelihood, but the Lord will provide hidden manna for their faithfulness.

What blasphemy is it to create a cross like the Patriarchal, placing Jesus Christ below a representation of the Catholic synagogue of Satan? What blasphemy is it to call any human of sin Holy Father? It is a blessing that Candlestick Pergamos—thou in which are not also known as—is still illuminated, while the secret groin of the Great Whore births a false illumination—illumination minus on equals the false illumination—fecundated after coitus with the Pope: prince of the power of the air; continuously and arrogantly blowing the Candlestick that keeps their secret alive.

<u>Five Hundred and Eighty Five Days</u> marked approaching destruction, an epoch in Columbia Babylon's history. Two doctrines created by the Catholic Synagogue of Satan has finally resulted in a conveyance of a warning with a sharp doubled

edged sword, sermonized by Pastor Booker and inspirited by Yeshua. The preachment would come to pass on television via MusaSatellite; Yana spoke first representing Pastor Booker's Co Minister, esteemed appropriate due to her expertise in the doctrine of Balaam.

"There has been a stumbling block laid before you, and only One man can reveal the truth. What stumbling block is considered the doctrine of Balaam? Look towards the Middle East, what group is using the Beast to demolish the leaders of Nations surrounding Israel, and afterwards will threaten to trample through the holy temple? Are these deaths coincidence or is there an administration involved? To find the answer look towards him that supposedly desires to make peace amongst the Nations of the world. Look towards him that will accept a Nobel Peace Prize. This Nobel Peace Prized candidate will take extreme measures to please those who are not pleased with other countries, even if they are upset with 'his own.' However, is 'his own,' his current place of kingship, or that place in which he is truly at heart from?

'Peace my brother to the Middle East! My Brotherhood consists of all religions, all races, all sexual preferences, and all political parties. Let's come up with a plan together to solve the economic situation, I am willing to listen to all suggestions.... or am I? All nations we need to unite! Unite! Unite!' Do these words sound familiar? Or do you not recognize them because they lack political nomenclature infusion? 'If you do not wish to provide a plan … wait a minute … what … you did provide a plan you say … sorry I didn't get that … well my plan will work just fine, and if you do not agree, my executive order overrides your opinion. I am the King of kings, what I say stands. What … you are Congress … well I am over the Congress, not the other way around. And since I am over the Congress the Average Joe definitely has no say.' This is what the forefathers of Columbia have planned since the creation of the New World, and soon the Prostitute will drown on the Island in which she currently stands.

Columbia, congratulations, you have your king of kings and placed his father at the top of the Pyramid. Now let's see how you survive with God Almighty's face turned away from the land. My people get out of her! The Lords judgment is at hand! I was blessed upon the Lord's coming Kingdom before He made His second coming known to man, and what royalty have I seen! There is nothing like dwelling in His presence. President Yeshua will soon reign for one thousand years, Hallelujah I say. Yeshua is the only One that can provide true change," Yana preached. After Yana addressed television land via MusaSatellite with a Pastor Booker style of preachment—preaching in the form of questions, Pastor Booker prepared to end with his conveyance of a warning with a sharp doubled edged sword to the churches characterized as Candlestick Pergamos.†[15]

"I am Pastor Booker the new aged Apostle John. I also have come to speak on behalf of the Son of Man, King of kings; the One who has ordained my tongue to speak with a sharp doubled edged sword. This is to the church formally known as Catholic. Your high priests have called themselves Holy Father, and in addition have placed themselves above Alpha Omega. Respect their current title on earth but stray away from their teachings. They have blasphemously equaled Allah to God Almighty when the spirit speaking through Allah was not the Spirit of the Lord.

If Jesus isn't considered the Son of God in the Quran aren't the teachings of Allah antichrist? Your high priests have blasphemously created an image of Emmanuel after a fornicator, encouraging the image to be graven into a statue to be worshiped. Would not their created image graven into a quote unquote Jesus statue attempt to make the blind bow? They have attempted to equal Bishop Sinterklaas—who by the way was worshiped—to Emmanuel; mocking the Lord by using Ho, ho: a

15. Revelation 2:12

115

term the Lord used in Zechariah Two:Six, telling us to flee from the land of the north. Do you get it, North Pole? In which is Babylon. Get out of her, flee from the St. Nicolaitans.

In Jeremiah Ten the Lord instructed us not to learn the way of the heathen, but the Synagogue of Satan incorporated the cut decked tree and a recreation of Bishop Sinterklaas into the celebration of Emmanuel's birth. And don't get me started with the bishop miter. Anyone like to play chess? The chess board is equivalent to the pyramid, both divided into four main levels. In the pyramid the god in which your high priest trust is at the top: the all Seeing Eye: the serpent, looking over the chess board which is earth, interrelated with your high priests as the Bishops. Second you have Aristocracy and Royalty representing those who rule: the Kings and Queens. Third you have the Horses, in which consists of the Bankers, Secret Societies, and anything Government. Last but not least is the bottom of the pyramid: everyday people, working as the Pawns. In chess you have the Bishop, Kings and Queens, riding in on white horses like they are Gods, contributing to the additional three crayoned horses of the apocalypse: red, black, and pale; using us as the pawns. Instead of washing your feet like our gracious King of kings: King of them, they throw the Pyramid and Chess Board in our faces on movies and music videos. Like chess there sometimes has to be sacrifices in order to win the New Ordered game.

Flee from their teachings and the Lord will provide you with a new name, disassociating you from the Synagogue of Satan's characterization, and into Emmanuel Catholics: like Saul was rechristened Paul. Flee from their teachings! Only confess your sins to a priest as a second form of prayer; the first form should be your confession and repentance to the Lord. For the priest alone is not a spiritual father, the Son is the High Priest. The serpent created the illusion that he is in complete control of the earth; saying 'obey or die from hunger.' However the Lord is in control of the universe and will provide you with hidden manna. Flee from their teachings, or you will inherent their lake of fire. God bless you all my brothers and sisters in Christ. For those of you who are watching and have not given your lives to Christ, allow Christ into your hearts, the end is near, the Light will not be amongst the earth long. Seek Blessings!"

Posterior to the live taping, Yana absconded back to the Jerusalem to continue her assignment in the construction of the third temple, amid Pastor Booker's avigation via Almsgiver to a forgathering including numerous pastors of mega churches. While Pastor Booker sat in the audience, one of the pastors/prophets prepared to administer a sermon about racism within the church.

"Good Dewy Eve my leaders in Christ, it is an honor to be amongst men and women that were clearly consecrated before birth to deliver God's word through the discernment of the Holy Spirit. We will read today from Acts Seventeen:Twenty-Three, Twenty-Six, and finally Twenty-Nine through Thirty; but in your own time I suggest that you read from Seventeen:Twenty-Two through Thirty-Four because the entire reading is valuable to the current topic. Let's stand for the reading of God's word, 'For as I passed by, and behold your devotions, I found an altar with this inscription, TO THE UNKNOWN GOD. Whom therefore ye ignorantly worship, him declare I unto you.' Now let's skip to verse Twenty-Six. 'And hath made—speaking of God—of one blood all nations of men for to dwell on all the face of the earth, and hath determined the times before appointed, and the bounds of their habitation' And we end with Twenty-Nine through Thirty 'Forasmuch then as we are the offspring of God, we ought not to think that the Godhead is like unto gold, or silver, or stone, graven by art and man's device. And the times of this ignorance God winked at; but now commandeth all men everywhere to repent.' Amen.

Now when I was in school my classmates considered me the reddest of the reddest red neck. I had my bald head, ignorantly wearing confederate flag shirts with the hat to match. Country defined my speech pattern and I analogously had a collection of black jokes. I always loved Jesus and possessed a big picture of what I was taught was Him on my wall, right between my 1969 Dodge Charger number seven poster and Nazi symbol poster.... You should see the way some of you are looking at me, if I did not feel protected by the Lord I would secretly find a way to the nearest exit," the Pastor humorously laughed as he continued, "No but seriously, we are all related, and not only by becoming born again through Christ, but brothers and sisters by Christ. The Lord stated in Acts Seventeen:Twenty-Six that we are all made of one blood. We all are descendants of Adam and Eve; however the bible does not reveal their completion. Studies prove that original man is of African descendant, but most pictures of Adam and Eve in books were of Caucasian completion. Whatever the case, humans created studies, science, etc. trying to reveal the mysteries of life; but we have a book containing the words of God, correcting or proving any discovery determined by man.

Yes Jesus did walk the earth and therefore had a complexion. Thinking of the phase 'we are all made of one blood,' why not would an artist search for a description of Christ in the holy word, and base their artwork off of the description explained by God Himself? One might say, 'we originated from Adam and Eve, so why would we look at the description of Christ?' because in the beginning was the Word, and the Word was with God, and the Word was God; therefore when the Word was made flesh that flesh was original man, the original flesh of Adam and Eve: second Adam. Don't get me to preaching up in here today, ha, ha. John Fourtheen:Seven 'If ye had known me, ye should have known my Father also: and from henceforth ye know him, and have seen him.' The completion of Christ is described in Daniel Ten:Six 'His body also was like the beryl, and his face as the appearance of lighting, and his eyes as lamps of fire, and his arms and his feet like in colour is polished brass, and the voice of his words like the voice of a multitude.' Polished brass described in revelations is bronze. You can call bronze whatever race you like, but do not call it white, black, green, or purple, call it what it is, bronze; and if Africans completion favors bronze call us all Africans, because the word of God called us all one blood. So if you are a racist, repent, because you are in battle with your own race.

Take down the pictures of Jesus depicted only as a white man and replace them with a Jesus Cross. Seek the real face of Jesus so you will not follow a false Christ: one that was not resurrected and died for your sins. Repent as God has commanded.... Now I feel a presence in the room this evening.... I feel there is a man in the audience that is of great importance.... please stand up if this is you that I am speaking of ... I am hearing a name ... Bookman, Booker ... if this is you please come," preached the highly renowned Pastor, calling Pastor Booker to the pulpit; feeling the Spirit overtake his cogitation.

Pastor Booker walked up to the podium and the renowned pastor discerned that he was the man of great importance and humbly handed over the microphone; even though Pastor Booker was not as well-known universally compared to others in the audience.

"I am Pastor Booker, the new aged apostle John, and I have come on behalf of Him who hath his eyes like unto a flame of fire, and his feet like fine brass. I accession with a conveyance of a warning to the churches with the personality of Candlestick Thyatira.†[16] I have walked along side with the Lord and He never ceases to amaze me, especially in the way that He uses people for His glory. Pastor Townsend you delivered a great sermon, a sermon that is in relation to the word that I have been sent here today to convey.

16. Revelation 2:18

Yes we all are one blood, so why have our blood siblings covered with a white completion fought so eagerly to deceive their own kind? Referring to the 'bounds of their habitation' in Acts Seventeen:Twenty-Six, our white siblings broke the Second Commandment while in their own habitation and forced a false image of Christ onto their black siblings and siblings abroad habitation in order to place an higher rank on themselves without qualms, resulting in the impairment of their siblings self-esteem. As another result other doctrines were created or continued because siblings of other complexions could not 'seek after God Almighty and feel their own way towards Him and find Him' as their own, in accordance to their own habitation. In other words the Black sibling, Asian sibling, Latin sibling, Indian sibling, etc. could not find the Jesus within themselves, and they refused to worship a white Jesus, resulting in the creation or continuance of the following stumbling-blocks/religions: Islam, Judaism, Buddhism, and Hinduism, among others.

We are one blood; hence the concept of being Christian should not be considered a religion but a way of life for the human race. With that being said, our African American siblings who share a like resemblance to fine brass took ownership of the ghetto: in which takes the ownership of being last. So again I say. I have come on behalf of the King of kings, President Yeshua: Him who hath his eyes like unto a flame of fire, and his feet like fine brass. To our African American siblings, the Lord knows your charity, and service, and faith, and your patience, and your works; and the last to be more than the first. The ghetto/poverty has been related to you, and those of you who lived in poverty but knew you were rich in the Lord, you may have been mocked but were not mistaken, and you will soon be first.

Notwithstanding the Lord has a few things against thee. You have allowed the prostitute to influence you to sell your soul for riches, for this you have no excuse. All of the following the African American brother has done without repenting:

degraded your women, worshiped your money, destroyed lives from selling drugs, cursed out your mothers and fathers, abandoned your children; all of the following the African American sister has done without repenting: prostituted your temple, entertained with sorcerous perversion by unnaturally revealing the flesh, aborted your children, worshiped your money; and in result you both have cursed your children.

The Lord will kill your children with death: which is the fiery lake; and you all will know that you are being judged by God, and He will give you also to the fiery kingdom in which your father-elect dwells, unless you repent. But unto the rest of Candlestick Thyatira, since you refused to sell your soul for riches, the King of kings will give you power over the nations: you shall rule them with a rod of iron, and smash them like potter as you please. Lord Yeshua will give you authority like He received from the Father, and also will give you the morning star.

To the mega churches in attendance; why deny an individual who is unemployed the word of God because they are unable to pay a tithe they did not bear? Or why convince an individual to give their life savings in order for you to profit from the Lord, while you—Pastors and leaders—do not give your correct tithe? I ask you, which is more honorable to the Lord: A man who makes a million dollars a week and provides a tithing of one thousand dollars; or a man who makes ten dollars and provides a tithing of one? This is equivalent to the Rich Man and Lazarus tithing at the same congregation. Past this message to our African American siblings through the wide audience in which you reach; nonetheless, few of you should also be held accountable: dancing atop offering at the altar, stating that whoever does not pay tithes should be shot; you are no different than the our African brothers killing for drugs, or African sisters unnaturally revealing their flesh. Therefore repent, or you will join your father-elect in his fiery kingdom. This advocate may sound unmusical but the Lord has had enough. God bless you all. Seek blessings!" Pastor Booker preached; and swiftly exited the forgathering.

Post hoc Pastor Booker's preachment, the room transformed into a chaotic state as all Pastors and leaders from mega churches across the world participated in a reciprocally clustered reaction, falling under a group that: dropped to their knees in repentance; proudly walked towards the exit without a desire to repent, analyzing themselves a better fit to be the new aged Apostle John; prepared to reach the lost as instructed by gathering their belongs and rapidly leaving the forgathering; talked amongst one another with disbelief; left the forgathering with the intentions of continuing to use God as a form of prosperity. Regardless of which group a pastor and/or leader epitomized, all in attendance discerned that Pastor Booker was truly sent by the Lord, and all, therefore were warned.

Candlestick Sardis bore multiple personalities through the medium of spiritually seven candlesticks: Ephesus, Smyrna, Pergamos, Thyatira, Philadelphia, Laodicea, and last but not least Sardis: bearing thine distinct candlestick; videlicet, the seven Spirits of the Heavenly Father dwell within Candlestick Sardis, while the seven stars represent the seven angels in which the Father uses—periodically as a rod—in order to correct what is not just. Experiencing the Father's discipline, a church christened Catholic Church of Christ adopted Candlestick Sardis†[17] after the Home Going of a specific soul.

Catholic Church of Christ was founded in Nineteen Eighty Three by Pastor Wicker Franklin. Born Nineteen Fifty Two in Cleveland Mississippi, Wicker Franklin grew up fortuneless in a family free from the teaching of racial discrimination; disregarding the imbuement displayed within a town saturated with racism. Witnessing the racial discrimination in his town, Wicker desired to make a difference: first becoming an

17. Revelation 3:1

Emmanuelist, and later deciding to attend Catholic University of America to eventually build a church. After graduation—CUA Class of Nineteen Seventy Three—Wicker Franklin became Pastor Wicker Franklin, however, not before the Holy Spirit appraised Wicker befitting to covey preachment.

Godspeed after Blessing, Blessing after Godspeed, in due time Pastor Wicker Franklin was blessed with a congregation as Godspeed became reality: ten Twelve Months after commencement. At the age of thirty one Pastor Franklin began his contribution to the Kingdom of God with the personality of Candlestick Philadelphia:

Love was displayed as soon as one would step into the first two doors of Catholic Church of Christ, continuing through service and upon the exiting of the first two doors following service. The Godlove†[18] promulgated was embraced by the members who attended, aggrandizing Pastor Franklin and leaders within the congregation: The Charity because of Pastor Franklin's love for people, displaying gentleness and goodness; Labor in building and maintaining the church through the faith/love for God; and Patience through longsuffering and faith/love displaying joy and peace knowing that the Lord would fulfill His promises: manifested Pastor Franklin's kingdom on earth, continuing whenever he would pass into heaven.

Through the transition from a community church to a mega church, Pastor Franklin encountered many investors sent by the serpent because of his honorable influence on the community. Several investors were a part of conflicting doctrines including Judaism, Mormonism, and surprisingly the doctrine of Yakub—a form of Islamism. In every meeting with an investor, Pastor Franklin opened with the same question, "In detail, who is Jesus?" following the open-ended question, "Describe the spiritual and physical characteristics of Jesus Christ"; in re-

---

18. [goh-duhv] the love in God revealed within another individual, passing that love to others

sponse, those investors who were a part of anti-Christ doctrines exposed the true intentions for their proposed investment based on their interpretation of the truth. After previous meetings in the months passed with various religionist including Mormonist and Islamist, Pastor Franklin evangelized following the meeting with a Judaist, preaching in relation to Christ and the law of the Old Testament.

"How is vitality with Christ my brothers and sisters?" the church replied "blessed" combined with a "Hallelujah," or "Amen," simultaneously as Pastor Franklin continued, "Let's start with our congregation's aphorism in reminiscence of Jesus' blood: for He accepted crucifixion for mankind's sins: because of His love. Stand while we give honor to the Lord by showing love and giving honor to all mankind. 'We are all one blood, made from the image of God Almighty our Father, let no doctrine made by man deter us from the teachings of the Lord: Jesus Christ our savior, Amen.'" After thousands of members synchronously quoted the churches motto Pastor Franklin continued with his sermon.

"I usually do not mix business with family business but I want to confide in those who I call my family, and in addition, my business experiences tie into today's sermon, Amen," the church responded amen as Pastor Franklin continued his speech, "The word up-to-date is in reverence to Matthew Five:-Seventeen through Nineteen, to also give honor to the Lord let us stand for the unmistakably certified holy text. I read today from King James.... I will wait while you all find the verse.... Again we read from Matthew Five:Seventeen through Nineteen. 'Think not that I am come to destroy the law, or the prophets: I am not come to destroy, but to fulfill. For verily I say unto you, Till heaven and earth pass, one jot or one tittle shall in no wise pass from the law, till all be fulfilled. Whosoever therefore shall break one of these least commandments, and shall teach men so, he shall be called the least in the kingdom of heaven: but whosoever shall do and teach them, the same shall be called great in the kingdom of heaven.' Amen.

There were many religions created before Jesus walked the earth and many evolved afterwards. Conformably, many religions have adopted the teachings of the Old Testament. However JESUS.... came DOWN FROM HEAVEN to save the world. Save man from the creation of any religion that was incorrect. Save man from darkness into light. Save man from any religion that would lead them into damnation. Jesus came down to confirm what religion/teaching was the only way of life, the only way to the truth. From the beginning of time, Adam and Eve, man was created to talk with God Almighty, to learn from God Almighty.

Therefore it is understandable how men yearn or have yearned to talk with, hear from, and learn from God but was deceived by the serpent; like Eve was deceived from the beginning. But JEESUUS.... came DOWN FROM HEAVEN to save the world. Superman is a comic book, Batman is a comic book, and Spider-Man is a comic book, but JEESUUS ... IS IN A BOOK CALLED LIFE, AND HE WAS NOT DRAWN INTO CREATION BY MAN, BUT JEESUUS ... HAS BEEN WITH GOD ALMIGHTY IN THE BEGINNING OF TIME, BEFORE GOD CREATED MAN.†[19]

Therefore my brothers and sisters do not be deceived. In John Fourteen:Six, Jesus states that He is the way, the truth, and the life: no man cometh unto the Father, but by Him. BELIEEEVE ... these words, I will not disparage any religion or religious leader, because this is not in the Lords teachings to do so, HOWEVER ... I will provide mankind with—regardless of their personal beliefs, the truth."

Eight Hundred Eighty Seven Days au courant: Pastor Franklin sermonized for over ten years—maintaining Can-

---

19. John 1:1-5 and Genesis 1:26 - "Let us make man in our image," us referring to Jesus.

dlestick Philadelphia—while his son Wicker Franklin Jr. pro-rogued under his wing. Unfortunately for Catholic Church of Christ, Pastor Franklin Sr. passed into his kingdom in heaven, while the church under Pastor Franklin Jr. adopted Candlestick Pergamos, and therefore officially became Candlestick Sardis; and therefore-squared, Pastor Booker was inspirited by Yeshua to sermon a conveyance of a warning, reminding the congregation of their personality of the past: Candlestick Philadelphia, that died, and of the Candlestick: Sardis, that now lives.

"Considering that I now speak on the pulpit of the once highly favored but currently expurgated church of Philadelphia: now Sardis, I see there is hope because of your Pastor's discernment of my obscured individuality. But for those of you who are without discernment I am Pastor Booker, the new aged Apostle John and I come on behalf of the King of kings: President Yeshua: the One that possesses the seven Spirits of God, and the seven stars. Pray for and receive discernment from the Holy Spirit: determining the Shepherd's voice from the serpent's voice; pray for remedy from blindness regarding your spiritual oculi, and thereafter be watchful. Pastor Franklin Jr. aka Jr. Pastor, you was raised in the church of Philadelphia under your father; so why have you settled for church Sardis?

The Lord realizes that you are in a different time from your father—obvious because of your Jr. Pastor alias—but this does not excuse your sacrifices in order to save New-Aged†[20] souls. The name of your congregation is Catholic Church of Christ. What is the definition of Catholic? (Liberated from pre-judgment; willing to sacrifice in order to please others; broad-minded). However your father accepted from the Lord a new name. Revive your father's unsacrificeableness. Work towards embodying the personality of church Philadelphia like you was taught as a child. Repent! Plant a tree bearing the fruit of the

---

20. [noo-eyj] the era of human esprit that are influenced by the New World: the Great Prostitute

Spirit and plant it adjacent to your first two doors. Prepare your church members and leaders as if they all would die tomorrow, whereas the Lord could come upon you all unexpectedly like a thief in the night. However, some of your members remember your father—the great Pastor Franklin Sr. teachings, and have held fast; not defiling their garments: like your father they also will walk with the Lord in white, for they are worthy.

Do not take for granted the father in which you were blessed. Repent, and restore the congregation that your father created: making Church of Christ the antagonist of defilement, with confidence that Jr. and Sr. will be printed in the book of life. May the Lord bless you all through these trying times, seek blessings," Pastor Booker preached, swiftly exiting, as the church pondered.

Perfection is impracticable in regards to trespasses due to one's birth into sin, notwithstanding, the Lion of the tribe of Judah: the Root of David: is the Vine of perfection. Since He is the Vine, and the church the branches, those branches can possibly bear a perfect fruit. Moreover, there is a church bearing the perfect fruit in a world of imperfection, adopting a specific characterization: Candlestick Philadelphia, but without He that holds the key of David, perfection again becomes impracticable.

The church in which possessed Candlestick Philadel-phia†[21] was like that of Catholic Church of Christ, but it knew not defilement. An olive tree represented the congregation's emblem: the root of the tree was labeled Root of David; the truck was labeled the Father; the branches were labeled Emmanuelist; and the olives were labeled Holy Spirit Love, Holy Spirit Joy, Holy Spirit Peace, Holy Spirit Longsuffering: Patience, Holy Spirit Gentleness, Holy Spirit Goodness, and Holy Spirit Faith. Picture the perfect television family and St. David & Trinity would represent the church version of that family.

21. Revelation 3:7

Every human race in existence had a separate section dedicated to their own habitation during praise and worship, however during prayer and the word everyone gathered together in harmony for the same teaching. The churches environment was full of love; it was prone for a member and/or leader—regardless of their race—to call one another brother and sister, accosted with a smile. In church meetings disagreements were settled with a five step peace reconciliation targeting forgiveness:

1. **Forgive and you will be forgiving**

   Matthew 6:14-15

   For if ye forgive men their trespasses, your heavenly Father will also forgive you: But if ye forgive not men their trespasses, neither will you Father forgive your trespasses.

2. **A lesson about forgiveness**

   Matthew 5:23-24

   Therefore if thou bring thy gift to the altar, and there rememberest that thy brother hath ought against thee; Leave there thy gift before the alter, and go thy way; first be reconciled to thy brother, and then come and offer thy gift.

3. **Forgive and Forgive and Forgive Anon**

   Matthew 18:21-22

   Then came Peter to him, and said, Lord, how oft shall my brother sin against me, and I forgive him? Till seven times? Jesus saith unto him, I say not unto thee, Until seven times: but, Until seventy times seven.

4. **Rebuke and Forgive Anon**

   Luke 17:3-4

   Take heed to yourselves: If thy brother trespass against thee, rebuke him, and if he repent, forgive him. And if he trespass against thee seven times in a day, and seven times in a day turn again to thee, saying, I repent; thou shalt forgive him.

5. Jesus is our Shepherd and forgives

Luke 23:33-34

And when they were come to the place, which is called Calvary, there they crucified him, and the malefactors, one on the right hand, and the other on the left. Then said Jesus, Father, forgive them: for they know not what they do. And they parted his raiment, and cast lots.

Nine Hundred Twenty Eight Days au courant: Considering that St. David & Trinity was a church of all races and habitats conceded in accordance to Belial's "E Pluribus Unum" plot, directed towards the continuous establishment of a New World. Correspondingly the Belial administration appointed innumerable investors in order to unclose—by the fornications of the Great Prostitute—an open door. However, innumerable attempts were unsuccessful due to Pastor Perkins' patience, with faith, knowing that his longsuffering would lend to the open door established by the Lord that no man could shut.

Following St. David & Trinity's entrance into the Lord's blessing—entrenching a mega church by overcoming longsuffering with patience—Pastor Perkins built a luxury apartment complex for less fortunate families. Regarding the application, in most cases the rent was negotiable and all prospective tenants' criminal background was analyzed in order to keep the property and environment elegant. Due to the economy the agreed upon rent was considered late by the tenth of every month, and payment prolongations were an option. At a disjointed location the church also constructed a homeless shelter containing a rehabilitation center and berth acquirer office—aka an employment office.

Pastor Perkins opened a coal company named Diamond Energy, erupting into existence to provide jobs for individuals with criminal convictions, offering over and above minimum wage. Occasionally—more-often-than-not—employees with criminal backgrounds are not treated with respect, but the management team analyzed their employees' family: displaying gentleness and goodness. A planet made of diamond was the company's emblem: including within the designs subsist a pulsar forming into existence the diamond planet.

Although Pastor Perkins loved emblems he did not acquire any graven images of Christ within the church, and slightly debated the leaders regarding the placement of a Jesus cross astern the pulpit. In conclusion, the Pastor ultimately agreed to place the cross behind the pulpit as a reminder of Jesus' sacrifice, exhorting the leaders and members against the slightest desire to worship the cross upon contemplation; instead offering an alternative: instantly think of Jesus Christ and His love.

Ensuing many years of benevolence Pastor Booker was inspirited by Yeshua to sermonize a conveyance of felicitations to St. David & Trinity's Pastor, leaders, and members; encouraging them to stay strong whereas their works were not in vain. Pastor Perkins was no stranger to discernment, realizing that Pastor Booker's visit to St. David & Trinity was no coincidence, vouchsafing Booker to take the pulpit for a word.

"Your walk with God has been long and trying, moreover, with longsuffering induced by patience endures success more abundantly: this is in relation to Proverbs Twenty:Twenty-One, an inheritance gained hastily in the beginning will not be blessed in the end. Your Father, my Father, knows best, so why do many avoid the wisdom in which we were blessed? We have many examples of quick success on television regarding movie 'stars' and music 'stars,' many have gone crazy, ruined their lives with drugs, including many other negative results, but all in one way or another will not be blessed in the end if they have not waited for success from the Lord. You—Pastor Perkins, leaders, and members, have applied this teaching within your ministry and in addition has applied it to your lives. You will soon be crowned!" Pastor Booker preaches; the church slightly interrupts with claps, Amen(s), and Hallelujah(s) as Pastor Booker continues, "I HAVE COME ON BEHALF OF He who is holy, He that is true, He that hath the key of David; what door He opens no man can close, and what door He closes no man can open.

Your opened doors have not been closed, for the serpent's helpers have little strength. You have been tempted, but passed the test. You have been persecuted, but passed the test. Your faith has been pushed, but not moved. Your gentleness and goodness has been tried, but you have not failed. You have forgiven with love and joy and choose peace over disharmony. You have come THUS FAR, so let no man steal your crown. There will be a great tribulation bequeathed upon the inhibiters of the earth after the Lord's face is removed; I can hear the Lord say 'I will not be amongst you long' and like a thief in the night He is gone, with you, St. David & Trinity, as well as some of His other most faithful on earth. Behold, you now come in the clouds, and those from the synagogue of Satan that persecuted you, and tested you, will soon worship before your feet knowing that the Lord loved you.

Envision First Kings Seven:Twenty-One, 'And he set up the pillars in the porch of the temple: and he set up the right pillar, and called the name thereof Jachin: and he set up the left pillar, and called the name thereof Boaz.' The Lord will make you as a pillar, to His left and to His right, provide you with a new name, and Behold, you will come in the clouds with the Lord in the middlemost: as New Jerusalem, tempted no more by the sin of this world. You have found your blessing! HALLELU-JAAAAH, HALLELUJAAAAH," Pastor Booker preached with towering excitement. The church shouted Hallelujah along with Pastor Booker, and he swiftly departed the church.

Candlestick Laodicea:†²² Shots fire as Pastor Brown and some of his leaders absconded Club Reverie at twilight on a Sabbath Day before Sunday; following the sound of vociferating tires indicating that the perpetrators fled the scene. Mildred Quisenberry—an ecdysiast at Club Reverie and church member at Millennium Baptist—hid in the back of the club along with her colleagues until the pandemonium ceased; while the bouncers expedited to the parking lot where the shots occurred. Fortunately after the bouncers fine-combed the anterior of the club there were no signs of injury. After the chaos ceased, Mildred called Pastor Brown to make certain no one was injured, fortunately-squared Pastor Brown and the church leaders safely departed.

Service the following Sunday at Millennium Baptist transpired like usual as Pastor Brown prepared the sermon to be ministered, while the praise and worship team blessed the congregation with psalms. Habitually the Pastor approached the pulpit at the last song to sermonize a sermon influenced by the Spirit of Truth.

"The word on the street is that I only preach about prosperity, but I have a word to shut the mouths of my haters. Yes God did bless me with a castle in the sky and luxury vehicles, but why not would a son inherent his Father's Kingdom overflowing with riches? Anyway I am going on a tirade again, forgive me Father in heaven," Pastor Brown states as an intro to his preachment.

Suddenly Pastor Brown began to pray with his head bowed performing a Raising Hands Gesture, while quoting a word from Second Timothy Two:Twenty-Three through Twenty-Six; and afterwards he comically collects himself to give the word encouraged by the Spirit of Truth. "For foolish and unlearned questions avoid, knowing that they do gender strifes. And the servant of the Lord must not strive; but be gentle unto all men, apt to teach, patient, In meekness instructing those that oppose themselves; if God peradventure will give them repentance to the acknowledging of the truth; And that they may recover themselves out of the snare of the devil, who are taken captive by him at his will. Amen! That verse was off topic from today's message, but I had to provide myself with a little wooosah, quoting a verse that God provided me on one occasion, before having a discussion with a hustle atheist....

Church I want to give a word today inspired by the Holy Spirit. This will not be a normal sermon today. So if you think you are not ready for the truth leave now, because it's going to get a little ugly in here this morning. This morning I want to talk about money," Pastor Brown laughs as he continues while the congregation sighs like not again, "No, no, no, there go the haters, ha-ha-ha, no but today the word comes out of First Timothy Six:Ten through Twelve, a verse that has been misunderstood for centuries. 'For the love of money is the root of all evil: which while some coveted after, they have erred from the faith, and pierced themselves through with many sorrows. But thou, O man of God, flee these things; and follow after righteousness, goodliness, faith, love, patience, meekness. Fight the good fight of faith, lay hold on eternal life, whereunto thou art also called, and hast professed a good profession before many witnesses.' See, people misquote the words in the bible saying 'money is the root of all evil' and not only fail to leave the phase 'love of money' out they also do not read the posterior TEXXT. Our Father wants the best for us. He does not want us to: Sell drugs for quick money, or; Sell our bodies for quick money, or; Sell our souls for quick money. He wants us to wait on HIS blessing, and the door He OPENS IN THE ENNNND, no one physically or spiritually can close. Not the devil, not the serpent, not Lucifer; not his servants, NO ONE. See, I was going to keep this to myself but ... I went to Club Reverie last night yall."

The church stared with disappointment and responded

with judgmental interjections as Pastor Brown continued, "See, I knew I would get that response, but the Holy Spirit told me to give the testimony regardless of the judgmental reactions. As a matter of fact ... I think I heard one of Tupac songs. What does it say? 'Only God can judge me now.' Yea there go the haters again. But no, I went there to evangelize the very word that I provided to you all this morning. It hurt my heart to see women take off their clothes for money. Stripping is not the 'good profession shown to many witnesses' mentioned in Timothy. This is exactly the type of profession ..."

Before Pastor Brown could finish his sentence Mildred Quisenberry stood up with a fracas outburst, "No, no, no Passta, you was not only 'evangelizing,' you was lusting all over Sparkle. Yea I seen you Passta, and I was ashamed. Don't come up in God's house acting all 'righteous' like First Timothy Six-:Eleven, when just last night you was showing Mammon what you got. Yea, strippers know the bible too. Matthew Six:Twenty-Four, 'No man can serve two masters: for either he will hate the one, and love the other; or else he will hold to the one, and despise the other. Ye cannot serve God and mammon.' Yeeaaa Passta, you and some of your road-dogs in the church was lusting over Sparkle, Bambi, and Tee Tee, so which master are you serving today with this lie?" Mildred—embarrassed due to Pastor Brown's Stripper comment—interrupted: in a disrespectful paroxysm, as Pastor Booker entered Church Millennium Baptist. Pastor Booker proceeded to walk through aisles dividing one section of the pew, leading directly to the altar, with his voice projecting just as loud as the microphone on the pulpit.

"Pastor Brown, do you know why the Holy Spirit encouraged you to reveal your whereabouts on your especial Sabbath Day: the day of rest according to your particular schedule? Jeremiah Six:Fifteen—So maybe you would blush, and fill convicted of your abominations. In lieu, you exalt yourself higher than a member in the congregation in which you minister? I come on behalf of the Amen, the faithful and true witness, the beginning of the creation of God. Church Millennium; as I speak to your congregation, pastor, and leaders I hear the name Laodicea, Laodicea; which is the Spirit of Truth revealing the characteristic of your church.

Mildred Quisenberry you stand correct, not in the way in which you confronted your Elder in Christ, but in your acknowledgement of the two masters worshiped in your church: God Almighty and Mammon: making your church neither, hot nor cold; 'I will spue you out of my mouth' saith the Lord with a thundering utterance: a doubled edged tongue. Millennium Baptist, you say that you are rich, increased with goods, and have need of nothing; I beg to differ. First Timothy Six:Ten through Twelve: Why do you not realize that you love your money? You hold your noises up high in the sight of the homeless; when the homeless should be the witnesses of your good profession. Matthew Twenty-Five:Fourty-One: Why do you not realize that you love your money? You refused to cloth the Lord when He first clothed you.

There is a trying time coming amongst those who are not rich in the Lord; those who have not learned to seek providence from the Lord. Your Mammon will abandon you in this time; he is a Seeing Eye Serpent: leader of the blind. Open your eyes! Look! See! Only follow the Shepherd, which is the Light. If you do not repent and turn from your Mammon he will leave you miserable, and poor, and blind, and naked; because under him your riches will soon mean nothing, only the Lord's Kingdom will survive in these trying times. Some followers of the Seeing Eye Serpent will commit suicide after killing their families because of Mammon's death; be grateful that you have a God that lives forever and ever. Repent! Do not take the Lord's forgiveness for granted. As many as He loves, He rebukes and chastens. I am Pastor Booker, the new aged apostle John, and I have come on behalf of President Yeshua. Repent, to seek blessings!"

<u>One Thousand Two Hundred and Sixty Days</u>: Pastor Booker continued his expedition across the globe via the Almsgiver with a conveyance of a warning to the churches with the personality of Candlestick Ephesus, Smyrna, Pergamos, Thyatira, Sardis, and Laodicea; excluding Philadelphia who received a conveyance of felicitation. While the serpent continued on his mission to infernate Jehovah-image's before time was up, many churches sought the blessings conveyed by Pastor Booker, and many fell within the serpents snare: for both, the Lord conveys the following message beginning with Reproaches: His mercy: "Behold, I stand at the door, and knock: if any man hear my voice, and open the door, I will come in to him, and will sup with him, and he with me. To him that overcomes I will grant to sit with me in my throne, even as I also overcame, and am set down with my Father in his throne.

Clause 5
Novus Ordo Seclorum Entertainment

Ere One Thousand Two Hundred and Sixty Days

Miss-conception wears a differentiation between motion pictures and the world news; however Mr. Parallel denudates lies for truth, primping Miss-conception with a clothing line branded Both Tell Half Truth.

One Thousand Two Hundred and Sixty Days: prophetically: As mainstream media spruces up with gustocarn†[01] via their reward for participating in the Great Prostitutes fornications—covering up unethical wars and unethical war tactics following the scapegoating of a witness, supporting that which is an abomination to the Lord while demonizing those who teach against the abomination, assisting in the agenda to control people by promoting gun control; Belial finally becomes the best-selling author among many presidents by writing and signing into law an executive order against "home terrorism" patented the National Defense Authorization Act (NDAA), in order to quote unquote prevent negative energy that could possibly create a terrorist mentality within Columbia: blocking authentic media sources provided through the internet that revealed or reveals the leaders in government unconstitutional legislation.

Numerous movies continued to entertain the masses using symbolism to reveal the next major catastrophe, while others indirectly revealed the truth regarding previous catastrophes. As the writer and the director deliver a quote paralleling,

---

01. [guhs-toh-kahrn] luxury or designer cloths preened to please the flesh.

"It's just a movie, produced to relieve the mind of its everyday trepidation": publicized repetitive sayings or messages uncover nefarious agendas. Alternative movies openly or symbolically encourage the audiences' flesh to act out that which is a secretly desired abomination or encourages the creation of a desired abomination; and or encourages one to accept or adapt to a soulinjurious situation, message, image, et cetera, presented within the motion picture.

Mainstream music artist evolve into Top Pawns in relation to the Contributors of the Chessboard, revealed by their invitation to perform at Belial's special accusations, inspiring to play a part in the New World's anatomy: a secret mouth. Unclean spirits like frogs speak with their tongue to magnetize their listeners, bragging in their videos or on stage with the use of Chessboard designed floors because they diligently kiss the feet of the Horses; but not all have to sell their souls to the serpent for a successful music career, however for those who have—and have avoided the Mark of the Beast—there is still little time left to diligently seek God Almighty and repent.

Moreover Contributors of the Chessboard and Top Pawns consider themself gods, and as the Top Pawns blasphemously label their albums a title equivalent to "God I Am" and idiotically use Psalms Eighty Two:Six through Seven a Psalm/Song from the Lord to justify their blasphemy, they mock themselves: "I have said, Ye are gods; and all of you are children of the most High. But ye shall die like men, and fall like one of the princes,"†⁰² says the Lord, satirically calling them gods, poetically expressing they are not God and they shall die like men and fall like one of the princes of the earth. However they know not, neither will they understand; they walk on in darkness: all the foundations of the earth are out of course, experiencing a falling away—paving the way for the son of perdition, departing from the faith, giving heed to seducing spirits, and doctrines

---

02. Psalm 82

of devils.†03

A Psalm/Song to the New Babylon of Columbia: "In the Lord put I my trust: how say ye to my soul, Flee as a bird to your mountain? For, lo, the wicked bend their bow, they make ready their arrow upon the string, that they may privily shoot at the upright in heart. If the foundations be destroyed, what can the righteous do? The Lord is in his holy temple, the Lord'S throne is in heaven: his eyes behold, his eyelids try, the children of men. The Lord trieth the righteous: but the wicked and him that loveth violence his soul hateth. Upon the wicked he shall rain snares, fire and brimstone, and an horrible tempest: this shall be the portion of their cup. For the righteous Lord loveth righteousness; his countenance doth behold the upright,"†04 saith the Lord:

Holy Spirit Translation: "In the Lord I put my trust:†05 how can you say this to my soul? Flee as a bird to your mountain.†06 Because the wicked bend their bow, they make ready their arrow upon the string,†07 that they may secretly†08 shoot at the upright in heart. If the foundations be destroyed, what can the righteous do? The Lord is in his holy temple, the Lord'S throne is in heaven: his eyes behold, his eyelids try, the children of men. The Lord test the righteous: but the wicked and him that loves violence his soul hateth. Upon the wicked he shall rain snares, fire and brimstone,†09 and an horrible tempest: this shall be the portion of their cup.†10 For the righteous Lord loveth righteousness; his countenance doth behold the upright." saith the Lord.

---

03. 1 Timothy 4:1
04. Psalm 11:1-7
05. Money - In God We Trust
06. Revelation 6:16
07. arrow on Columbia's Secret Seal
08. Secret Societies moving towards a New World Order
09. Revelation 6:7, Revelation 9:17, and Revelation 19:20
10. Revelation 17:3-6 and Revelation 18:4-6

Though ye offer me burnt offerings and your meat offerings, I will not accept them: neither will I regard the peace offerings of your fat beasts. Take thou away from me the noise of thy songs; for I will not hear the melody of thy viols:†[11] the song lover says to New Secular with wisdom, and an interchangeable sacred writing reads: Be not conformed to this world: but be ye transformed by the renewing of your mind, that ye may prove what is that good, and acceptable, and perfect, will of God:†[12] Amongst your brethren and the world become a trendsetter, no more an imitator; your eminence will encourage others to follow: flee from the serpent's snare and yoke to an empyrean monarch: God's Kingdom.

<u>Two Hundred Fifty Five Days</u>: As Faye O transitioned into a viol of eminence pleasurable to Yeshua—Godhead—many fans rejected her new style, while her genuine fans remained loyal; withal, every apostate fan was replaced by two God fearing fans. While Faye O toured across the globe, paparazzi expanded as rumors continued to circulate suggesting that Parousia was upon the world; desperately attempting to capture a photograph of Yeshua. However, eventually, the rumors were put to rest: although Faye O completely changed her rhapsody, attitude, and raiment—shirts imprinted: "Jesus saves"; "Hell is real, repent"; "The Father's daughter"; "To the serpent: If Jesus is the snare, I'm the drum."—she was never seen accompanying Yeshua on a photograph.

Although Taye Boii presently did not manage Faye O they remained in touch as associates. Like old—before she temporarily converted to the serpent—Faye O, on several occasions, endeavored to convert Taye Boii to Emmanuelanity.

"You are my girl and all, but ... you could not afford me now Faye O, because I know you are not getting to the money like you were before. You know ... going back to Christ and all,"

---

11. Amos 5:22-23
12. Romans 12:2

Taye Boii told Faye O over the phone, as she attempted to convince him to be her manager only as an attempt to save his soul.

"If you only knew," Faye O responded as Taye Boii continued:

"Ok, I will make a deal with you. If you can show me the books from Sally the Accountant proving that you make just as much as you did before. I will work for you again," Taye Boii states; mesmerized by mammon.

"I mournfully wish that I could show you the books Taye Boii, nonetheless ... I will not convince you to save your own soul with paper-specie.†[13] We hold people lives in our hands, are you not slightly concerned about the people we have affected with that music?" Faye O stated with fretfulness.

"All I care about is getting to the money, I'm not concerned about my soul; much less their soul, financial situation, nothing; as long as they can buy the album (what they use to say) we Faye O over here; if it don't make Money Banknotes why print it? You use to be down Faye O. Why are you politicking with me about management anyway? Oh yea ... ha-ha-ha, you hurting over there financially that's why you mournfully can't show me the books. You want another taste of the life don't you?" Taye Boii laughs as he rambles, "Well you know how the verse goes 'You can't serve God and money' or 'You can't be hot or cold, be one or the other' Yeeea ... well you better stay hot over there, because we are cold over here; heart ice cold getting to the diamond gold; and if I burn in the afterlife, this life was worth the ride."

Faye O begins to tear up before Taye Boii could end with his last sentence. Excluding the remarks directed towards Faye O their conversation resembled the norm—before she temporarily converted to the serpent; however her cry was for Taye Boii and the snare in which the serpent trapped him. After this

---

13. [pey-per-spee-shee] a slang word for money.

particular conversation with Taye Boii their conversations altered to limited, and limited developed into nonexistent.

The stage name "Faye O" was universally a house hold pseudonym, and interviewers were competitively interested in her episode on stage while singing "Jesus Think I'm Sexy" and even more interested in her near death experience. Faye O finally decided to do an interview with a famous female journalist named Dolores Buchannan to explain her recent memoirs. The interview was broadcasted while walking through Anaheim California.

"So this is your stomping ground, Anaheim California?" Dolores asked in an attempt to be Hip, walking with Faye O through her hometown.

"Yep, yep, the Heim is my hearth, birthed and raised," Faye O responded with comicalness.

"It must have been nice growing up in the city of Disney World, Disney World every Saturday, eh," Dolores states.

"I wish, we grew up in the slums, yes, we did and still do have projects in the original, yes original, city of the Angels: quote unquote Anacrime. No, but unfortunately, we never had enough money to alight from our little lime Hoop-Dee Chevrolet Camaro LT and land in Disney World," Faye O responds.

"Well, with your current financial situation you could buy Disney World, I postulate.... Well ... we all know why you're here, fans want to know about your recent happenings on stage; but let's begin with the most important question: Have you found Jesus?" Dolores asks, generally disinterested, but leading to a point in the interview that would make the conversation more interesting to Faye O's fans of the past and future.

Taken aback from the question asked by a known atheist, Faye O squinched her eye lids and slightly pulled back her head while looking at Dolores. "He, actuallly found me, and picked me up while I was in a terrible state; it was like I was Lois Lane and

He was my Superman," Faye O passionately states with humor.

"So, you are suggesting that He picked up you in the spirit correct?" Dolores responds, with a confused and yet inquiring facial expression, confident that the answer to her question would be yes.

"No, I mean Jesus physically picked me up and healed me," Faye O responded escaping from her normal jocoseness.

"I don't think that I am following you," Dolores Replies with an inquiring mind, covering up her inquiries with the stare of unbelief.

"The cameras may not have revealed this, or knowing the broadcasters they edited it out, but Jesus PHYSICALLY picked me up and rescued me from Vicky, Mikey, and Damon. I always knew that they were controlling my decisions, and it was kind of freaky, but I loved the fame and financial stability. Damon use to help me write my lyrics. Mikey and Vicky was a couple contributing to my swag on stage and in the atelier: where I painted a picture on the instrumental, ha, you know how I do. No, but seriously, after they left I realized that I did not need them and the talent was there all along, a gift straight from the Creator," Faye O ended, worshipingly dazing after discussing Jesus.

"All Greek to me," Dolores replies, using an idiom as the synonym to Not Again; giggling: "L-O-L, anew!? Vicky is a new one," Dolores states, sarcastically joking while rolling her eyes before continuing, "Now you know my intentions are not to insult you Faye O, because please understand that you are my favorite pop artist without puzzling over; but, Mikey!? And Damon!? Without irony, these are names we have not heard as of yet. Moving on ... ha-ha, let's discuss your near death experience."

"Well ... I am not a snitch so I can't tell the full story, but let's just say I was betrayed by someone who I thought was a true friend; I guess that I was mistaken. Anyway, I always knew in my heart that the only way out of my music deal was through death. This was just understood when I began to establish myself as one of the greatest and most rotated pop artists. Long story short, when I died I went to the pit. However when I was there, I knew that Jesus did not rescue me to let me remain there. I just had an unexplainable faith that He was coming to my rescue in the process of my death, and when my death actually occurred: sending me to the pit, I still knew He was coming," Faye O explained with a stare of discomfort.

"So ... what do you mean by the pit? Hell? And if so describe the pit to your fans: I included," Dolores states with a puzzled stare.

"Yes I was in Hell. It is not a place that I would wish on Mini Redbone, and you know how we can't get alone," Faye O slightly jokes but immediately straightens her smile to a serious grimace and discombobulated stare. "No, but, I would not wish that punishment on my greatest enemy. As a matter of fact— you being my friend—we have to talk later off the record, no DJ chop/no joke, no joke. The screams were unbearable; all senses were at full blast, more real than life on earth. Physical beings have not experienced reality until they encounter the spiritual world," Faye O analyzed as the interview came to an end.

Following the interview Faye O proceeded to evangelize to her atheist friend in an exertion to salvage her life from the beast of the sea. Not interested in Faye O's conversation Dolores Buchannan nonchalantly proclaimed that she had a prior engagement and must be going: the typical response as tears dropped from Faye O's pupils once again, concerned about the lost souls from her past and her inability to assist in leading them to the Light.

Four Hundred Sixty Seven Days: The music awards could not persevere without one of their biggest artist, therefore Faye O was guaranteed an invitation to attend: conjointly reassured a solicitation considering that she was a potential nominee for best song of the year. Initially wanting to disassociate herself from the snarartist†[14] of the music industry Faye O contemplated her absence, but Yeshua convinced her to attend in an attempt to unshackle a snared soul.

While Faye O remained seated, convinced that she would not be chosen for best song of the year: due to her opposition to the serpent, the live award show progressed as artist from every genre performed their latest hit incantation. Directly before the announcement of best song of the year, four bestselling artists from genres Rhythm and Blues (male: Shah Heav), Rap (female: Mini Redbone), Pop (female: Babae), and Rock (male: Rascal Hill) performed their major world premier collaboration "Rain Man Rain":

Darkness surrounded the stadium as the stage's lighting formed a pyramid. Initially sharing one sixteen bar verse, each artist revealed themselves one after another (only while performing their particular verse): by falling from the celestial designed ceiling into the top of the pyramid, descending to the bottom of the pyramid, and landing on the chest board designed stage floors. After the last artist descended to the bottom of the pyramid and ended their verse, the quartet proceeded to collaborate on the chorus.

On the chest board stage Mini Redbone and Babae both performed wearing one eyed masks with horns like a Bongo to represent the baphomet; additionally Mini Redbone sported a black horse tail and white laced shirt imprinted with a RFID chip logo stating "chip in"; while Babae sported a pale horse tail and black laced shirt imprinted with an identical logo. Shah Heav wore an expensive white suit, ankle wrapped goatskin shoes (representing the baphomet), a gold RFID chain, and a white horse tail; withal, Rascal Hill wore an expensive red suit,

---

14. [snair-ahr-tist] a person who sacrificed themselves, to the serpent's snare, in pursuance of professionalism affiliated with one of the preforming arts: music, dance, theater, etc.

goatskin cowboy boots (representing the baphomet), a cowboy hat imprinted RFID, and a red horse tail.

When entering onto the bridge of the song a bugle band accompanies the quartet following the rampage of United Nation dressed soldiers; the performance ended with the chanted chorus while the soldiers pretended to apprehend the four major recording artists. Faye O, completely knowledgeable of the satanic symbolism within the performance and song title experienced a state of embarrassment and outrage, as snarartist and a partially bewildered crowd cheered in abundance.

After the world premier collaboration Gina Breeder and Freddy Hampton—two internationally known movie stars—prepared to announce results for best song of the year. Songs from four potential nominees—including Faye O's "Jesus Think I'm Sexy"—displayed on the stages mega projector before the results were revealed. "And now without further ado the best song of the year is awarded to ... Faye Oooo, Jesus Think I'm Sexy but I'm not impressed," Gina Breeder announced, simultaneously singing while reading the results, as Freddy Hampton simultaneously quoted the title of the song along with a segment of the chorus.

Faye O headed to the stage with her new entourage to accept the award, smiling while hugging Gina Breeder and Freddy Hampton, as her yeshuanity controlled her true feelings. "First and foremost I would like to thank God Almighty in Jesus' name for the opportunity to stand before you all cauterized by death: resurrected born again. With that being said, this is to those who consider themselves the Chief One's of Isaiah Fourteen:Nine, devotees of the Chief musician and Angel of Music weakening the nations. I am embarrassed, ashamed, and outraged by the diabolical rituals performed here today, in a deliberate attempt to mock the Creator of you all's existence.

It sickens me that I used to be a participate of this music, and as horrible as hell was I now feel blessed for the experience because it was well deserved considering that I was a participate. You all know my ex-personality, and I am not going to lie, it would be nice if I could go back one second before Christ and curse you all out for disrespecting my Father; but that also would make me a hypocrite considering that I am on stage to accept an award from a song of my past entitled "Jesus Think I'm Sexy."

Unfortunately but fortunately I am going to have to renounce this pyramid shaped award and my blasphemous song. God bless you all, and no matter what the Angel of Music tells you; as of yet, it is not too late to repent," Faye O wows the crowd from her normal "thugged out" aggressive styled—but now slightly altered—speech pattern and walks back stage where like Déjà Vu the body snatchers of her past anticipated her arrival to complete their unfinished business.

Suddenly Yeshua and Kirtana appears; Yeshua, disrupting the body snatchers' path with a Thundering Accent, "As many as I love, I rebuke and chasten. I have showed mercy on you two once before, but in that meeting you confused my mercy for weakness: in that meeting you two were warned Faye O was mine and you would surely die awaiting the first terror; for I am not man, that I should lie: therefore today is the day that you will meet your father elect, in his fiery kingdom."

With warning the body snatchers dropped to their knees bowing while their souls screamed for mercy looking up at Yeshua and their bodies. Both souls blaspheme Jesus as demons entertained themselves with their new personage: picking apart their limbs and chopping off their necks, just to connect them back to dismantle again: reiteratively. After the event back stage the crowd felt a sense of uneasiness following Yeshua's voice thundering throughout the stadium: "What fool worships the musician but mocks the Creator of the ear? One designated for a fiery hell indeed. For Idols are sheep leading sheep, wondering from the Light into darkness." Nevertheless, without repentance, the award show continued through snared delight.

♪ JESUSOVERIDOLS ♪

Two Hundred Fifty Five Days: Rachelle—Foxy Fox—continued by expanding her show Christian Talk, launching the show from the palace in Washington District of Columbia. As the host of her new improved format, Foxy Fox employed two hilarious female comedians turned Emmanuelans to eminently spice up the show. Christian Talk was exceedingly capable of becoming a morning show, but Foxy Fox wanted the show to proceed in bewitching hours to quote unquote Fight off the Harlot Vampires—spirit of whoredoms—attacking young woman after the club.

Nine Hundred Thirty Days: While other radio stations promoted the presidential debates, Foxy Fox focused on Yeshua, not only because Jehovah is a jealous God, but she was prophetically acquainted with the Spirit of Truth—as well as Kirtana and the twelve Devotees—knowing that ultimately Belial nor the "potential" replacement for beast out of the sea would prevail as president: administering the victory to Yeshua: One Thousand Two Hundred and Sixty Days. Moreover building the kingdom—by directing women off of the street towards Christ—was incontrovertibly more paramount than any presidential debate.

Four Hundred Seventy Days: "Sex or the Comforter" was a show topic of great interest and controversy, attracting the sinner by the phase "sex," however chaperoning the listeners to—pardon my French—comme il faut conversation; debated by critics because the topic's "out of the box" ethos. "Foxy Fox and the Comediennes" focused on the topic for the third time due to its popularity as well as importance in relation to leaving the club's atmosphere.

"Microphone check-check this is Foxy Fox and Comediennes:

'Michelle-Michelle'

'And I'm Vania aka God's gift russian-on-ya,'" Foxy fox
states, following Michelle-Michelle and Vania's announcement
of their own names, as the trio contributed to the normal introduction.

"Again we are on the topic Sex or the Comforter which
has been a heated discussion recently, because the world's media
acts as if we as Emmanuelan's do not live in the world as well;
basically suggesting that we should not even mention the word
sex much less hold a discussion on the topic," Foxy Fox states
as Vania interrupts:

"Well if they need help getting over it Balaam can tell
them what they can take the stick out of; or better yet what they
can talk to before kissing."

"A little over the top Vania," Foxy Fox responds while
interrupting Vania, jokingly but however with a slight tongue-
lash.

"I apologize boss lady, still walking in my deliverance; Jesus knows I didn't mean any harm," Vania states as her voice
change painted a picture of her looking up. Observing Vania,
Foxy Fox and Michelle-Michelle began to chortle.

"You are a silly one V-V, seriously," Foxy Fox states while
continuing to chuckle, "But zealously, right now I want to go
straight to the callers. If you have been pressured into sex for
a one night stand after the club or if you are currently in a sexual relationship with a man out of wedlock please call in, One
Eight Six Six Talk G-O-D or One Eight Six Six Eight Two
Five Five Four Six Three. This is for my Queens around the
world, whether you are in a committed relationship or you have
just seen a gorgeous man at the club smelling like Clive Christian—the smell of riches, offering you a ride in his Bugatti. No

price is worth your soul; call in, One Eight Six Six Talk G-O-D or One Eight Six Six Eight Two Five Five Four Six Three. Let's talk about this thing my Queens," Foxy Fox states as Vania replied, "Hmm Hmm Hmm," and Michelle-Michelle replied, "yes-yes," in response to Foxy Fox's mentioning of Clive Christian, imagining the cologne's pleasant smell on an attractive man.

The lines flood as Foxy Fox selects a random caller. "Hel-looo Foxy Fox and Comediennes," the woman says with a Latin Accent as the trio responds back with their own unique greeting. "I know I am a Queen from the Philippians but what if I just can't fight the temptation. I mean, I have been in a relationship with my man for two months and I have not giving up—what I call—the confection, if you know what a mean. We have did a little something-something here and there but we have not taken it to the max. I don't know how long I can hold out. I mean we are in love, so doesn't that count for something?" The woman states rapidly, searching for a prophetic answer.

"Yes my sister you are a Queen, so don't let any man riding and dying with the Adversary take your crown. You and I know what I am talking about regarding your man and the Adversary, so I am not going to put your business in the street. But the Comforter will fulfill any loneliness or physical eagerness until you are placed with your rightful mate," Foxy Fox states with discernment leading into Michelle-Michelle's comedic response.

"Kick that Buster to the Trap and make him ghost like that movie—I don't mean to tell my age yall—but when they say who you gonna call, tell'em Tyrone but you can't use my phone, fake pimp be gone. Your goods—or confection—appertains to your future husband. See my girl Foxy Fox and I have a different style of prophecy, I will put your business out in the street messing with me; ha-ha-ha, but it's all in fun. Listen baby, I know you don't know, but your man has a wife, and about three kids. See, he went down there to the church house and got him a Christian girl, thinking that church girls were easy. That man could care less about the Father, much less you; he is just looking for some tail and willing to wait for you only because of the challenge. You are a Queen; hold tight to the Comforter so that you can: keep your crown in the Kingdom," Michelle-Michelle stated using the word "can" for the beginning of a cadence in agreement with Foxy Fox's "take your crown" statement.

While in the palace Yuhann Shareef—who is considered an Adonis—made a guest appearance on the show to discuss his position on the topic: explaining how he waited a year to have copulation with his significant other; in particularly until she became his wife. The lines ensuingly denatured from a flood into a tsunami with women that were inspired by Yuhann's testimony, inquiring to inherit inspiration in order to save themselves until marriage: breaking any generational curses. Additionally young women called into the show inspiring to unravel the secrets of their significant other, and ask Yuhann for advice regarding their relationship from a man's point of view. Supporting Foxy Fox and the Comediennes, Yuhann conjointly became an antagonist of the women's significant other: convincing them to wait until marriage in order to avoid fornication.

Five Hundred Eighty Days: Weed vs. the Spirit of Truth was also a topic of great interest and controversy. Foxy Fox, Michelle-Michelle and Vania experienced the side effects of smoking weed thereafter understanding the comparison between weed and the Spirit of Truth.

"Mic Microphone check-check this is Foxy Fox and Comediennes:

'Michelle-Michelle'

'And I'm Vania aka God's gift russian-on-ya'.

This is part three of Weed vs. the Spirit of Truth in which like Sex or the Comforter has been a topic of great controversy, but again I am not concerned about the haters, I will continue to broadcast any topic that the Holy Spirit leads me to discuss because no one else holds my salvation: with that understood here we go," Foxy Fox states disparagingly, understanding the influence that the serpent has on the show's critics.

"I use to be a ganja smoking Rastafarian until I was released from the snare by way of the true Light. Back then people use to ask me 'Why do you smoke weed?' and my response was 'It opens up your mind by way of enlightenment, you wouldn't understand until you have pulled one ya hear; and in a way that is the truth, the same half-truth spoken by the serpent who deceived Eve, saying that her eyes would be opened and thereafter know good and evil, if she would eat the fruit; weed is a representation of that very fruit. Ganja is not only a gateway to other drugs; ganja is a gateway to beguiling spirits: spirits that know the truth but purposely twist the truth. Once the smoker's temple is in an intoxicated state these spirits even have the ability to speak through the smoker.

Most of the lyrics in the songs today are not written by the artist but by the beguiling spirits or spirit themselves: one of the greatest tricks of the serpent/former Chief musician of heaven. However through the Holy Spirit comes true enlightenment. The Holy Spirit will provide the whole truth; the Spirit is a professor; and the Spirit will give you a high and knowledge that no "blazing of that fruity" can provide. In referencing the serpent, Eve and the forbidden fruit: you tell me if it is a coincidence that fruity is a slang word for a type of weed," Foxy Fox states in one segment of the show, providing her testimony and revelation revealed through the Holy Spirit, following Michelle-Michelle and Vania's comedic response. Withal, Faye O made a guest appearance on the show via cellphone supporting Foxy Fox's statement regarding evil spirits, assisting in the lyrics of artist after smoking weed.

<u>Four Hundred Seventy Days</u>: After the show Sex or the Comforter, Yuhann, Faye O, and Foxy Fox—as motivation to

counterattack—administered their focus onto the video entitled "Rain Man Rain" staring Shah Heav, Mini Redbone, Babae, and Rascal Hill; filled with satanic symbolism showing reference to Rain Man—the serpent "pouring down blessings":

Lightening falling from heaven near a picnic table in a beautiful rainforest set the video in motion. In an evening setting, four scenes flash as Shah Heav, Mini Redbone, Babae, and Rascal Hill are revealed sleeping in a location separate from the rainforest—specifically in the downtown area of their big city—with newspapers used as a blanket covering their clothed bodies; along with a "Will work for food" sign, propped against a grocery cart full of their belongings. Suddenly rain drops in the four big cities following the opus, as the four artists began their mission in search of shelter from the rainfall.

"Will work for food" sings a different tune: "Will work for shelter," divulged on the artists' signs while they continued to beg self-aggrandizers, unwilling to lend a hand. Supernaturally, rain falling on the four artists turn into money and money into white tailor made garment; after the money formed into garment that completely clothed the artists, suddenly a sparkling glow surrounds them as the money transformed back into normal rain: shadowing the bridge of the song.

Night falls: Leading into the end of the song another supernatural event occurs as the four sparkling artist teleport: simultaneously walking from their big city into the rain forest. Downpour chaperoned the artists into the beautiful rainforest as they look around in amazement. Suddenly two scenes flash following the sound of thunder; one scene reveals a lion on the picnic table and the second scene reveals an owl in a tree. Forthwith, the four artists walk towards the picnic table covered with a thanksgiving feast, shielded by an umbrella imprinted "Will work for food" and "Will work for shelter." The four artists assist one another in dislodging the umbrella; after the umbrella is removed from the ground Shah Heav launches the umbrella abroad; concluding the opus: as Shah Heav, Mini Redbone, Babae, and Rascal Hill proceed to eat the thanksgiving feast in the rain.

"Coincidently" following the Rain Man Rain video, Dolores Buchannan interviewed a new pop singer named $ummer. In the interview the instantaneous top of the chart artist explained how "It was like yesterday" that she was homeless, and suddenly in result of an Artist and Repertoire named Dr. Matthew she became famous and rich overnight. Dr. Matthew who discovered her playing the guitar for food felt as if she had "the look," and named her $ummer—meaning the rain only last until the sun shines. $ummer also spoke in regards to how she was Faye O's biggest fan, however stating that Faye O's time was up due to her change in music genre, arrogantly concluding that she was here to replace Faye O. Dolores Buchannan—acting as if she greatly enjoyed the interview—concluded that $ummer was her favorite pop artist. $ummer's interview entered directly into her new video entitled "Last Breath," a song encouraging teenagers to party irresponsibly until the world comes to an end:

The video begins with sunshine after a rain storm, immediately flashing into two scenes: the first scene reveals a rainbow and the second reveals $ummer with another woman puckering up to kiss at an after party; directly flashing into the next two scenes: the first reveals half of a party banner reading "Gay to see," a cutaway scene discloses a clock reading Eleven Fifty Nine and calendar reading December Twenty First; the next scene revealed the second half of the party banner reading "another day," and a cutaway scene discloses the clock at Twelve Ante Meridian with the calendar marked by an eye covering December Twenty Second.

Throughout the video inverted crosses are revealed—the exegesis of blasphemous mockery—dancing to the beat by flashing in and out between each scene; alike, pyramids are reveal along with one cutaway scene exposing the Skull and Bone logo. On a dance floor resembling a church altar, a "pastor" runs in and out of the scene's background, replacing the Jesus cross with the star of baphomet; while party goers dance with $ummer in the foreground. At the terminus of the video $ummer dances with an enthralling short dress designed as a Columbia flag. Exhausted by dancing, unable to breath, $ummer completely ends the video on a hospital bed—labeled Belial care— hooked up to a pulse monitor and the video ends with a flat line.

Seven Hundred Seventy Seven Days: Counterattack by exposure manufactured "The Initiation," a movie written and directed by Joannes Casting, staring Yuhann Shareef and Faye O. Yuhann and Faye O played two detectives turned conspiracy theorists who were ousted from their positions because they uncovered the secrets of a society that supposedly ruled the world. From different cities the two detectives "coincidently" meet and teamed up. Both still able to carry a concealed weapon, ready for any ordnance, endeavor to uncover unsolved crimes committed by the society and crimes in which the society used a scapegoat. Little did the detectives know the society was larger than expected; therefore the detectives searched for a team of gangstas turned Christians, willing to risk their lives for Christ in the fight against evil.

"The Initiation" competed with Numen Sirius: when Columbia suffers from the ruins of the Hoover Dam due to evil terrorist forces, Numen Sirius struggles against the forces responsible; saving the world from complete and perpetual destruction. Supreme Being reincarnated into a human, originating from the bestselling comic book, Numen Sirius is the hero readers long for as they desperately wait for the movie.

"Emmanuelan" protestors were created in an attempt to ban "The Initiation" from movie theaters; especially after it was discovered that the movie would box office obscene numbers, topping Numen Sirius—a movie financially supported by the in telligentsia, full of freemasonic symbolism. A Belial controlled media introduced the created hype regarding "The Initiation" worldwide. True Emmanuelist did not find any issue with "The Initiation" and actually considered it outstanding as construed from the box office numbers. YouTube views were also manipulated from The Initiation's movie trailers in order to reduce the blockbuster's promotion.

All efforts directed towards the incapacitation of Faye O's music and movies, Foxy Fox's radio show topics, Yuhann's movies, and Joannes' movies were rejected via Yeshua; convincing the serpent that Jehovah was still in control and time was almost up, entering <u>One Thousand Two Hundred and Sixty Days</u>.

Clause 6
The Secret Signet

Nineteen Fifty Nine Anno Domini the Secret Signet†[01] of "Solomon's" Hawaii was redesigned to announce and honor the approaching birth of a king. In plain sight symbolism mocks the blind eye as the Signet unseals an apocalyptic future: an eagle beholds the king, symbolizing that he is responsible for its lake of fire and brimstone; taking no notice toward the Great Prostitute in which it represents. Moreover portraiture of the sun epitomizes the Son of the Morning, peeking over a shield; Out of many, One: represents fifty states combined into one world, displayed within the shield.

Eighteen Sixty Eight Anno Domini the Secret Signet of "Solomon's" Illinois was redesigned into the second Great Seal; prophetically announcing a dwelling place of the king. A banner's grandiloquence declares, "The king lived here so this is his state," unsealed within the phrase State Sovereignty; refusing to allow the National Union Party to interrupt Columbia's original propose: indicated by the eagle's snapping of the beak in order to separate the banner. The shield gripped by the eagle is a retrospect of the Civil War and the reigning king of Eighteen Sixty One through Eighteen Sixty Five; the king of Eighteen Zero Nine through Eighteen Sixty Five also represents the penny (not pictured) imprinted with a like shield—Out of many, One; replaces the thirteen states—is a retrospect of a Second Civil War: Moreover portraiture of the sun epitomizes the Son of the Morning, peeking over a symbolization of the beast out of the sea.

Apropos of the Secret Signet of "Solomon's" Columbia: Working collectively, the king and the National Union Party formulate a professional wrestling styled storyline/plan to

01. Seal

shutdown Columbia in order to further indebt the country, preparing for the implementation of the RFID chip. Pretending to despise one another, headed towards campaign, the two parties use Belial care as their reason for struggle; while the Pawns of the Chessboard are forced to order the event via Pay-Per-View: infernatist panic, as the child of God assimilates that their economy is not of this world.

Ere One Thousand Two Hundred and Sixty Days

Equivalent to traveling through the country of Gergesenes— those who come from pilgrimage or fight; evil spirits were casted into the New Yorkshire hog, as the Pilgrims of the New World cursed while naming their biggest city. After New York was established the Great Prostitute relocated from Babylon New York via U Haul, compassing through biblical streets to reach her crowning destination: Babylon Farmington Rd, merging on Southern State Parkway blasphemously crossing over Jerusalem Avenue, exiting onto Cross Island Parkway to Long Island Expressway beginning to mimic the beast out of the sea, onto the Brooklyn Bridge, loving the sin that Eve created by biting the Big Apple to turn right on Adams street continuing on Brooklyn Bridge, confiding in the Recession to exceed the Great Depression in order to start a New Order while riding down Franklin Delano Roosevelt Drive, finally harboring on: Liberty Island New York New York, to officially parallel the beast out of the sea.

Nationalities from every Head†[02] travel abroad in the hopes of obtaining freedom, visiting the Prostitute as she states,

02. mountain or continent; Revelation 17:9

"Welcome Home," noticing her visitors from abroad look up at their Continental Head represented on her crown. It is a Mystery how a Seal sits on the King to the Mother of Harlot's immediate front, as the Eagle's eye spots the Seal and captures it while at the peak of the King's pyramid; the Mystery concludes the Abominations of the Earth, unsealing the Eagle flying away from an Olive tree, and towards an Indian shooting arrows. Towards the ten Kings in which she sat upon, the Great Prostitute was flagrantly offensive: scarlet colour, boastfully raising her arm without repentance holding a golden cup,†[03] filled with abominations and filthiness of her fornications illuminating like fire from netherworld; embodiment arrayed in amethyst.

September Eleventh Two Thousand One Anno Domini—in the year of our Lord: marked the coming and blueprint of the tribulation, as two figures designed like planes crash into twin buildings on Liberty and Church Street. Afore September Eleventh Two Thousand One Anno Domini the Great Prostitute could be found approximately ten minutes away from her residence planting explosives in a pursuit to destroy Church and Liberty. Triumphant in destroying the twin buildings and innocent lives, Mother of Harlot†[04] escapes and successfully reaches her residence unnoticed, continuing to boastfully raise her arm, replacing a scapegoat with repentance. As far as Church and Liberty, in the ruins a cross announced the coming of the King of a kings, destined to preserve the church and establish true liberty:

Satellites detect a light resembling a white horse rapidly traveling from the sky. The Axial Intelligence Agency determined the coordinates of the unidentified object along with its exact address and proceeded to apprehend the settled subject. A penetrating knock on the door eventually leads to the Brooklyn

---

03. Revelation 17:3-6, Revelation 18:4-6, Psalm 11:1-7 and President Yeshua - Novus Ordo Seclorum Entertainment: Page 166
04. the Great Prostitute daughter of the Great Whore

streets; two street walkers will become the witnesses for Ye-shua—the King of kings destined to preserve the church and establish true liberty—and will be blessed with abilities unparalleled from any corporeal entity.

Two Hundred Fifty Five Days: Before Kirtana was shepherded by Yeshua to Jerusalem along with Yana, Jock, and Ianto; Kirtana contacted the Fashion Squad to provide the Olive sisters with raiment made of sackcloth, designed in a variety of styles; the line of raiment was manufactured in a quantity of abundance, lasting One Thousand Two Hundred and Sixty Days.

Day One: Reveries became prophecy as Olympia and Shanese dreamed dreams. Taken aback by the dreams maturing into déjà vu, the Olive sisters consulted Yeshua in order to decipher their unexplained abilities installed into them by the Father. Yeshua's revelation humbled Olympia and Shanese inspiriting them to fisticuff with serpent spirits: even through death, similar to the Secret Service; in addition to the powers installed by the Father, Kirtana enrolled the Olive sisters into Martial Arts—practiced in conjunction: entering Two Hundred Fifty Five Days.

Two Hundred Eighty Five Days: After the Fashion Squad completed the fashionable line of raiment made of sackcloth, the Olive sisters learned to combine Martial Arts with their supernatural abilities and the necessary readiness for battle manifested. Sequentially, Olympia and Shanese traveled abroad in the hopes of emancipating the streets from Confederate Vampires—serpent spirits. Provided with discernment via Spirit of Truth concerning the plans of Confederate Vampires within Belial's administration, familiar with the livelihood of streetwalking, Olympia and Shanese pioneered their plagues—delivering women from the harsh New York streets—against Confederate Vampires in the "Capital of the World" nom de guerre home of the United Nations before applying their powers across Columbia and abroad.

Cimmerian umbra infiltrated the Big Apple's thorough-fare. A flesh peddler aggressively handles a group of strumpets while they attempt to flee. Shanese and Olympia pull up in a Bentley Mulsanne and roll down the window to confront the male perpetrator.

"I don't ever remember enjoying a man put his hands on me," Olympia stated to the flesh peddler, speaking from the passenger's seat.

"Nice car, but I think you went a little too far with the sackcloth outfit. Although I have to admit, you don't look that bad in it," the man states, wrapping his arms around two of the women necks while looking at Olympia as he continues, "Do yourself a favor. Stay out of pimping business unless you are willing to become a part of the flock."

Olympia opens the passenger's door and proceeds towards him as he releases the two strumpets. "I know you are not challenging me to a fracas?" the man laughs as he continues; "This must be persiflage." Without warning the man reaches for and grapples with Olympia's throat.

While Olympia looks into the man's eyes suddenly her throat replaces the flesh peddler as he uncontrollably strangles himself to his death with a bewildered stare. The group of strumpets gazed open-mouthed, striving to gather what their eyes conceived. After the flesh peddler collapses Olympia extends her attention to the group of strumpets.

"We are in the last days. Your temple which is the body is more valuable than medium of exchange. Think not of this world but of the spiritual world: for the spiritual is where you will spend most of your existence. Ask yourselves, would you continue to sell your temple if you inherited a kingdom? If the answer is no, repent, and turn away from your fornication and follow Christ before time expires. Believe me, I understand your situation but your jewels are priceless, give them to no one until you find a husband. If you need assistance off of the street contact the Olive sisters, we will provide you with a place until you are back on your feet," Olympia evangelized, handing out their contact information—business cards titled Olive Street Team—before entering the vehicle. Several strumpets admire the Bentley Mulsanne as Shanese departs, while others stare at the luxury vehicle inspired by Olympia's words.

The flesh peddler weathering the first plague happened to be Francis Clinton, the brother of a former king of New Babylon. After the former king was informed about the happenings involving his kin, suspensions of murder disestablished the autopsy results, indicating suicide; however lack of evidence ended the investigation.

The thing that hath been, it is that which shall be; and that which is done is that which shall be done: and there is no new thing under the sun:†[05]

Two Hundred Eighty Six Days: An African American man is flagellated lifelessly in the middle of Seventy One West Twenty Third Street New York New York, while pedestrians imperviously walk by as if the five transgressors and martyr were intangible. Without hesitation the martyr's Latino friend bombards the altercation as parallelism triumphs. Succeeding, a Bentley Mulsanne interrupts the utter confusion by the sound of a woman's modulation: contrasting the brutal scene.

"That is a terrible way to beat a man, even one excused of the worst crime," Olympia states in a soft voice catching the transgressors' attention. "I beg you, please let them be."

Two of the transgressors reply relatively simultaneously, "You have no business within this circle," the first man replies, following the second man:

"Yes mam, your best bet is to trek your pretty little car

and pretty little face elsewhere; so they both can remain as they are."

Shanese parks the car and walks around to the passenger's side and opens Olympia's door. "I am afraid that I cannot obey your request," Olympia states following Shanese's response, "Please, let them go. We only come out of love."

"We only come out of love too honey," the first transgressor laughs while responding, as the other four transgressors relieve the martyrs of their beating and progress towards the Olive sisters.

Rawhides advance towards Olympia and Shanese's neck released from the five transgressors. Utilizing their Martial Arts the Olive sisters counterbalance the lambasting by circumvention, resulting in a mysterious backfire and the decapitation of the five transgressors heads. The two martyrs could not believe their eyes, whispering to one another with a disbelief of disapproval as if the Olive sisters started the altercation, somehow forgetting that Olympia and Shanese came to their rescue.

The Olive sisters notice but nonchalantly ignore the martyrs' ridiculous reaction and look at one another in a titillated awe while entering the Bentley; still amazed and excited apropos of their abilities. Afterwards, pedal to the metal Shanese departed, and the martyrs contacted their attackers' next of kin in order to clear their names with regard to the murder of Kurt Harding, Kamp Wilson, Maco McKinley, Fairchild Coolidge, and Cady Truman: the five transgressors and clanspersons of five former kings of New Babylon. After the former kings of New Babylon descendants received details regarding the nature of their kindred death, suspicions of measure for measure haunted their supposition. However lack of evidence ended the investigation.

<u>One Thousand Two Hundred and Sixty Days</u>: prophetically: December Twenty Third Nineteen Thirteen Anno Domini, the Federal Reserve Act reasserted that the Thirteenth

Amendment was water under the bridge but however predominantly voided the Amendment by way of taxation: Uncle Sam took out a lawn from Columbia as Columbia became the shareholder of Uncle Sam's citizens. Promising a change, Belial—a representation of Uncle Sam—concocted a plan to eliminate the debit crisis by eliminating the Federal Reserve Act, reestablishing the Act through the RFID system; leading to Columbia's second Civil War: as Belial takes an arrow from the Secret Signet of "Solomon's" Columbia and sits on a white horse equipped with a bow,†[06] Yeshua states in a Thundering Accent, "The secret signet is misprinted; for the eagle looks towards war."

Two Hundred Eighty Seven Days: Emmanuel crosses burn at a campground in New York. Leading away from but adjoining the crosses, eight intellects gather surrounded by a crowd of thirty. Each of the eight intellects possessed eight different titles, separated into two groups, displayed on their tailor made butterfly collared suits: Intellect one, Goldman Sachs on the right wing and Rockefeller on the left; Intellect two, JP Morgan on the right wing and Rockefeller on the left; Intellect three, Lehmans of New York on the right wing and Rockefeller on the left; Intellect four, Kuhn Loebs of New York on the right wing and Rockefeller on the left; Intellect five, Rothschilds of Paris and London on the right wing and Rothschild on the left; Intellect six, Warburgs of Hamburg on the right wing and Rothschild on the left; Intellect seven, Lazards of Paris on the right wing and Rothschild on the left; and last but not least, Intellect eight, Israel Moses Seifs of Rome on the right wing and Rothschild on the left.

Welcomed due to the class of vehicle, a Bentley Mulsanne pulls into the campground's vicinity following Olympia and Shanese's presence walking towards the crowd of thirty eight. Captivated by the Olive sisters' beauty, the eight intellects and crowd of eminent supporters "blessed" the sisters with their attention by reaching for their wallets.

"This is a business proposal for your salvation, not your pleasure," Shanese states as the incantational†[07] phantasms flee.

Now grasping that the Olive sisters were not their erotic entertainment, the eight intellects belittle Shanese and Olympia with insulting confabulation, disrespectfully fondling the sisters while the group narrow-mindedly agglutinated. Not to be mistaken for profaneness Olympia and Shanese's thoughts connect, "Go to Hell," Shanese states:

As Olympia finishes Shanese's sentence, "all of you!"

In response to the Olive sisters rebuke the eight intellects and their followers began to laugh, continuing with their act of sexual harassment; suddenly Mother Earth opens up her fiery mouth and swallows every insulter.

Witnessing the eight intellects and celebrities plunge into the belly of Mother Earth, two wanderers rush over to the scene and instantly commute into the spiritual world; while the Olive sisters leer earthward into the abyss. Olympia, Shanese, and the wanderers witness the eight intellects and celebrities as they were torched by unwanted advances and disturbing laughter. Through discernment the Olive sisters realized that the incantational phantasms seen fleeing from their presence were the torchers along with other incubus.

Shanese drives afar while the wanderers proceed to enlighten the owners of the campground about the burning crosses in addition to their witnessing of the eight intellects and celebrities deaths. The payroll distributors—Federal Reserve Cartel—of nearly every king of Columbia heard about the gruesome deaths of their relatives and had an intuit of foul play; however lack of evidence ended the investigation—but the propinquity of the kings vowed to unmask the identity of the Olive sisters.

07. [in-kan-tey-shuhn-nl] of or pertaining to the success of incantation

Rikers Island would discontinue the Olive sisters' journey in New York, before traveling across Columbia and abroad. Inspiring to minister and not afraid of any man, the sisters felt obligated to beacon individuals experiencing Hades on earth to the Light, unearthing paradise after death. Indifferently encouraging evangelism, the warden welcomed Olympia and Shanese with open arms: persistent in a week long program entitled "Come out of her."

<u>Two Hundred Ninety Days</u>: While the prisoners filled the room Olympia and Shanese greeted them with genuine opened arms. The seats were half full as it became clear that no other prisoner was interested in attending. Olympia opened up the program with a poem in the form of a rap—while Shanese beat on a table—in order to keep the prisoners interested.

"Unconcerned about your life I'm the man on B Block. Teach you how to trap crack now you got that lock, teach you how to X-out your foe no prank-I got a drank we can bank on ladies with a tank top. Never mind about the man who created you. How is He real just look at where He got you: Locked up family could careless-whooo, will-give-you-work you a felon nooow. Move-the-crack cause I showed you hooow. Watch for the cops cause it going down. If you see a judge give your laawyer illumi pound-you out," Olympia raps; surprised by her ability to rap the prisoners indiscreetly cheered, capturing attention from the prisoners who choose not to attend.

Immediately Olympia begins to pray, and afterwards she continues with the program. "The fact that I received applause from that rap is just as blasphemous as the lyrics; therefore first of all I had to repent, even though I spit the verse to prove a point. Those twelve bars sum up the trash that you dump into your ear, breaking your self-esteem and character. Your favorite artist convinces you to destroy your life over a nice beat and you love it: nod your head to it, memorize the lyrics and repeat them. If only you knew the power in words. Do you not understand that God Almighty spoke the earth in which you walk on in existence? L-O-L Shanese I can remember the quote back in the day, 'Sticks and stones may break my bones but words will never hurt me.' Regarding this expression, nothing could be further from the truth. Whether you realize it or not my brothers, words plus thoughts equals the actions that have you locked up like the animals that you are not. Your favorite artist could care less about your life. They convince you to perform acts that they themselves would not perform. Even if they perform an illegal act they have the money and quote unquote hand signals to serve little time and be released: as a promotional tactic to sell more records.

Do not blame God for your actions, He is not the reason that you are here. You currently have adapted to a hell on earth because of the words installed into you by the serpent. See your favorite artist will go from a paradise in the physical world to a real hell in the spiritual world; but don't let them convince you to suffer hell in the spiritual in addition to the physical. If you have life in prison, which is a form of hell, make your qualms with God in the name of Jesus, so you can pass into a paradise after death," Olympia preaches.

Subsequent to the first meet of "Come out of her," prisoners vamoosed back to their cells while the only prisoner that did not cheer concluding Olympia's rap trudged behind the others. With discernment Shanese punctuated the prisoner's path through discourse.

"Why did you not cheer after my sister's rap?" Shanese asked the prisoner with discerntion†⁰⁸ as her consciousness takes the words out of his mouth.

"I usually am excited about hood rap verses, but when.... who is that, your sister?

08. [dih-surn-shuhn] to distinguish from the Spirit of Truth; addressing the person in which the information revealed was in regards to, in order to get an conformational replay.

...performed her verse it did something to me. I even liked your beat on the table, but it was something about the word's used in her rap. Yes it was the same message pounded into my head by some of my favorite artist, but her words made me upset because it was like she was talking down to me. Her tongue is very powerful," the prisoner replied, surprised but thankful that Shanese took interest in his demeanor.

"Yes her words are powerful. Take these sacred writings and read out of Revelation Eleven:One-Six. Between me and you it will reveal my sister's true identity, in addition to why her words are so powerful.... I see your number; but that means nothing to me or your Father in heaven; may I ask your name?"

The prisoner responds, "John," as one of the guards yells times up; following the Olive sisters' exiting.

Three days into "Come out of her" equiponderated to more prisoners as word spread through the Neoteric Long Island: equiponderating to universal grapevine telegraph. Concerned about the positive influence that the Olive sisters had on their prisoners/slaves, fifteen founders of the Corrections Corporation of Columbia (CCA)—Phoenix Washington, Gus Adams, Edwin Jefferson, Ryan Madison, Kevin Monroe, Weston Adams, Trent Jackson, Reese Buren, Russell Harrison, Garrett Tyler, Walter Polk, Miguel Taylor, Jeremy Fillmore, Jake Pierce, and James Buchanan—held a meeting at a disclosed location in order to discuss a plot that would silence the Olive sisters.

Two Hundred Ninety Five Days, the last diurnal course of "Come out of her," coincidently the fifteen founders of CCA designated John—following his reading of Revelation—the perfect scapegoat to commit murder because of his violent past; targeting the Olive sisters candidates for americide. Noticing that Olympia and Shanese's outfits were always designed with sackcloth and experiencing their forcible words, John realized the sisters' true identities and struggled with the thought of committing such a terrible act against two of God's chosen ones: however John's opposing thoughts convinced him otherwise, willing to sacrifice for the wellbeing of his wife and children.

Hours yore, leading to the beginning and last day of the Olive sisters program; all seats are filled causing some prisoners to stand behind the occupiers. Jehovah-images become Emmanuelist as the Olive sisters expatiate about God's kingdom. Inspired by the week long message an ex-murder now born again Emmanuelan raps about how Jesus saved his life. Olympia and Shanese smile while looking towards the entertainer: who has captured the attention of all prisoners in attendance. Taking advantage of the pandemonium, John grabs Olympia, draws a Twenty Two RTF, and holds it to her head while pulling her away from Shanese.

"I morn for your soul John, after your reading of the Holy text I know that you realize what you have gotten yourself into. The sacred text must not return void and must be fulfilled through manifestation; however ask God for forgiveness before your story ends. I cannot promise that all will be forgiving and you will stand beside the Lord. What I can promise is that your family will see no harm and their threateners will be exposed," Shanese states with no detected fear in her speech pattern, unmoved by John's violent episode but saddened by the current circumstance, while the prisoners stare in anger due to their respect for the Olive sisters.

Suddenly John is supernaturally dragged away from Olympia while he continues to point RTF towards her; unable to control his arm thereupon he points RTF towards his own head. Now in control of his embodiment, John realized the act in which he hazarded, disappointed and afraid of the consequences he pulls the trigger. "The primitive projectile is a blank," Olympia states before Twenty Two RTF speaks; instructed not to attend the program, guards now dispatch to the room after hearing RTF's voice.

John goggles the gun with a stare of stupefaction, surprised that he is still alive, following two prison guards tackling him against the floor. After Twenty Two RTF is thrown into the crowd of prisoners due to John's apprehension, a curious prisoner secretly obtains RTF, and shots the wall in order to uncover the bullet blank mystery. Abstruseness simplifies as the bullet partially damages the concrete wall following two additional guards apprehending the inquisitive prisoner.

Supervening upon apprehension of the two prisoners, news reports of the incident apprehends television. The fifteen founders of CCA were outraged after ascertaining that the Olive sisters were still alive, and rage evolved into lynching as "suicide" ended John's consciousness: nonetheless not before the publishing of John's "suicide" letter. To cover their tracks, the fifteen founders disposed of John's suicide letter—in which was incriminating evidence, and planned a vacation in Hawaii to celebrate their claim to be numina.

While sipping Pina Coladas and watching news the fifteen founders of CCA noticed John's wife on television holding up his "disposed of" and incriminating letter, proving that his alleged suicide was a case of murder. Suddenly fifteen cases of the gallows stormed Hawaii's atmosphere: the death of the fifteen founders—distant descendants of fifteen kings of Columbia—disturbed their kindred, indicting the cause of their suicides on Olympia and Shanese. In the interim, the Olive sisters traveled to Chicago, on a quest to relieve the streets of Confederate Vampires.

Jesus↑Over↓The Streets

The thing that hath been, it is that which shall be; and that which is done is that which shall be done: and there is no new thing under the sun.

<u>Four Hundred Ninety Five Days</u>: Prophesies from the lexeme of God continue to befall under the Belial administration in consequence of the Secret Signet of "Solomon's" Illinois—representing the state of a city flourishing with human trafficking: Neither shall he regard the God of his fathers, nor the desire of women, nor regard any god: for he shall magnify himself above all; Daniel Eleven and Thirty Seven's second prophetic topic heavily comes into existence.

Chicago hotels and abandoned houses encourage new aged slavery as signs labeled "Johns Only" symbolically reestablish Illinois Black Codes. A 1931 Duesenberg pulls up to one of the deserted houses following the exiting of the Olive sisters, Olympia knocks on the decrepit door while Shanese stands abreast. Disturbed by the unexpected hammering Abraham Johnson discourteously opens the door with fleetness, "How may I be of assistance," Abraham states with sudden courtesy, taken aback by their enticing sackcloth attire.

"I heard that you were the man to see for employment opportunities," Olympia states, tone paralleling her appearance.

"It depends ... are you cops?" Abraham asks with humor; however with a "but seriously answer the question" deportment.

Olympia responds, "No,"

In harmony, Shanese contributes to the sentence with, "we are not cops,"

"But we are interested in your line of business," Olympia states completing their sentence.

"With who are you two accompanied?" Abraham states; squeamishly checking his surroundings, surprised by his stroke of luck.

"We are led and chaperoned by the Spirit," Shanese passively states with the intentions of receiving a passive reply.

"Well ..." Abraham laughs, "I do feel like our spirits are connecting, please, I know it's not much but both of you ... make yourself at home," Abraham states while tossing disarray from the sofa onto a vacant chair's crest rail.

While the Olive sisters take a seat on the ostentatious sofa surprisingly matching the interior of the home, Abraham promenades to the upper story brandishing his arrogance, looking back with innocence in a stratagem to make the sisters feel comfortable. Anticipating their own capture, the Olive sisters provide a counterfeit screech after being snatched from the living area to the second story by two robust men.

Through the disturbing journey on the second story women in great numbers were divulged accompanying the rooms with their assigned Johns: invited by the invisible reestablished Illinois Black Code sign—clearly seen by the condition of the house's exterior. The Olive sisters were forced into a room occupied by six other women. On the outside of the room five men lined up anticipating the chance to winnow out woman, leading to their choosing. Olympia and Shanese convinced the first man to coopt them, refusing to bear responsibility for allowing the six women to experience sexual abuse in their presence. Agreeing upon their suggestion John one selects the Olive sisters; the Muscle forces Olympia and Shanese into the process of coition to boot.

Tout de suite, Andrew Lincoln bulldozes the Muscle and John away from the Olive sisters, "What ... Andrew? I don't know what your worriment embodies buddy, but a dire fish story is a sine qua non; no hoodwink," the Muscle states in an African French Accent, confused in reference to why his colleague acted as a vigilante. Withal the Olive sisters brought to bear their yeshuanity and shepherded the six women out of the room and out of their experience with the murk, while Andrew followed.

Revisiting the journey by exiting the second story became less disturbing: women began to follow the Olive sisters/lodestars after the sisters eclipsed their rooms, leaving the Johns and Muscle in every room befuddled with concern regarding their inability to control their own embodiment. After Andrew and the last woman exited the decrepit door Olympia and Shanese engaged in sympathetic introspection, and their thoughts of hell on earth engulfed the house with fire.

Consequent upon the conflagration, the Olive sisters pro-vided shelter and benefaction to numerous of the once captive women, helping others return to the family in which they were kidnapped. Andrew proceeded to the overseer of Operation Slave Trade while the Olive sisters continued on their steeple-chase in conquering Confederate Vampires/Apocalyptic Horses. Two additional kindred of two kings of Columbia experienced death following Andrew's visiting to the overseer, as news of Abraham's death enraged the overseer/kindred of Abraham: After days elapse, at the tomb engraved Andrew Lincoln, the overseer and accomplices discuss a plot to extirpate the Olive sisters.

Nine Hundred Seventy Seven Days: Sixteen distant de-scendants of sixteen kings of Columbia lay deceased "due to" the Olive sisters' journey throughout Columbia; in actuality the descendants' deaths were a direct result of generational curs-es owing to the descendants' inspiration to accomplish Colum-bia's original purpose: appointing the descendants Confederate Vampires. After completing their journey across Columbia the waters surrounding the Great Prostitute turned into blood,†[09] and the Olive sisters traveled to the third temple in Jerusalem to visit Yana; there, in the Middle East, the sisters would continue their prophecy and release any plagues necessary.

One Thousand Days: An explosive drone designed into a missile hits and causes the Hoover Dam to collapse. Millions were left without power while thousand's lost their lives. Con-trolled under the Belial administration the media reported the tragedy a terrorist act and deemed the Olive sisters the perpe-trators. Trusting on the Lord the Olive sisters accepted blame

09. Revelation 11:6

for the tragedy but however was puzzled as to why Yeshua allowed the tragedy to occur, leading to the following response from Lord Yeshua:

"People choose the serpent as their father elect but then ask how the Father in which they deny why; why is his discipline so cruel? Why does God in heaven allow such devastation? The Father protects His children on earth and the punishment for sin is death; therefore when a child of God faces death, do not worry, for their paradise awaits; however those who deny the Father selects devastation, and devastation is the serpent's offer indeed," Yeshua explains to the sisters in a Many Ocean Accent, relieving any ounce of doubt within the Olive sisters' apperception and planting their minds with the seeds needed in order to complete their prophecy: providing nutrients to those in which they would confront.

Cautiously—however dauntlessly due to their consciousness of the Father's protection—traveling throughout Israel and Africa the Olive sisters conveyed their prophecies, healing weary Emmanuelist with mental and spiritual nutriment. While covering ground in Egypt a vagabonded sorcerer confronts the Olive sisters amid evangelizing to impoverished tribes. Aware of the situation in Columbia revealed to him by a perverse spirit, the sorcerer questioned God's existence.

"How can your God be real, and if He issss, real, why do we live assss, we do? Why hasss your God allowed such devastation in Columbia, the land of the onccce free? I would not dare worssship, such an unconcern God. Why are you here? Your liesss are not welcomed within this land," stated the sorcerer with a Snake Accent, pronouncing the S in every word with a hiss.

"The last will be more than first; to answer your first question. I will not bother to ask what spirit you are operating under; howbeit for the sake of my sisters and brothers I will satisfy your inquest Mr. Coroner," Olympia states with humor, mocking the perverse spirit. "Repentance is needed in Columbia; many of the citizens without power have accepted Satan's gluttony, heavily drinking from the cup of fornication and abomination. Sex is exploited and enjoyed without marriage; worship of foreign gods is practiced and promoted; homosexually is promoted, same sex marriage is accepted; murder is entertainment: all without repentance. Those that acknowledge God exist choose Satan; so since God is a God of freewill they are released to a Satan entertained by devastation. Therefore spirit of perverse be gone in Jesus' name, I erstwhile identify your worthless identity." After Olympia's rebuke the sorcerer practically vanished, and the Olive sisters continued to supply their spiritual nutriment.

Plagues trouble Africa and Israel as well as the continent and country's endogenous King(s) "due to" the Olive sisters, expediting a meeting with Belial—who was in search of the sisters due to their dealings in the Hoover Dam tragedy. Periodically entering Belial in the past during his speeches, the Great Dragon ascends out of the bottomless pit to finally germinate in Belial's temple; as the Olive sisters travel to Calvary—also known as the Place of the Skull. After the sisters reached their destination and remained stationary in order to pray, Belial received word of their whereabouts and ordered a strike entitled King Bush.

Two Olive Trees/Candlesticks of Yeshua are dissevered from their roots on account of King Bush, necessitating another speech by the Beast, taking credit for while announcing the deaths of the sisters responsible for the Hoover Dam tragedy. Belial also announced that the bodies of the two perpetrators would not be buried beneficial to honoring those who lost their lives in Columbia.

Like a vintage clock the Great Prostitute continues to tick tock her snare, causing the world to participate in the rejoicing of her governmental scandal: while the kindred of Confederate

Vampires sent gifts to one another, the serpent achieves one of his last hemoglobin discharges concerning a child of God: as the voices of Emmanuelans cry—on behalf of the Olive sisters and themselves, "How long O Lord, holy and true, dost thou not judge and avenge our blood on them that dwell on the earth?"†[10]

One Thousand Two Hundred and Sixty Days: After three and a half days forwent, the Rerooter†[11] relit His two Candlesticks. When observing Olympia and Shanese stand to their feet after their cadaverous bodies lied in Sodom and Egypt—nom de guerre Jerusalem—for three days, excessive disquietude fell upon the eyewitnesses. Suddenly Yeshua stated in a Thundering Accent, "Come up hither," instantly Belial and the kings under Belial were in the spiritual world: and the current kings of the earth also witnessed the Olive sisters ascend to the third heaven via the ole buttermilk sky. Before denouement of the diurnal course a great earthquake occurred, shepherding the falling of Jerusalem's king and his administration—the tenth king under Sea Beast, following the deaths of seven thousand citizens, and the remaining citizens gave glory to the God of Heaven.†[12]

---

10. Revelation 6:10
11. [ri-roo-ter] the Spirit of life, holding the ability to revive that which is deprived of life.
12. Revelation 11:11-15

Clause 7
The Assembled States and Statue of Freedom

I Pledge Allegiance, to the flag, of the United States of America; and to the Republic, for which it stands; one Nation under GOD, indivisible, with liberty and justice for all.†[01]

My country 'tis of thee, sweet land of liberty, of thee I sing. Land where my fathers died; land of the pilgrims pride; from every mountainside, let FREEDOM ring.†[02]

When one pledge allegiance with God, and accepts Jesus Christ as their Lord and Savior, then comes their only chance of freedom. Only due to the grace of God has this land remained great—under the snare of the serpent. Unfortunately this land is not indivisible and will shortly be divided—under the snare of the serpent; divided like the word Religions†[03] due to the serpent, and due to the serpent's influence—on our fathers who died and pilgrims' pride; dividedly combined, into a New World: New Babylon.

Religions were not created to coexist, confirms the four beasts†[04] before the throne of the only Almighty God. The four beasts represent the gods worshipped on earth, worshipping the true and living God: extinguishing Emmanuelism†[05] as an offi-

---

01. "The Pledge of Allegiance," by Francis Bellamy. Youth's Companion. September 8, 1892.
02. Thomas Arne. 1831. "American (My Country, 'Tis of Thee)," by Samuel Francis Smith. Rare Book and Special Collections Division, Library of Congress.
03. [ri-lij-uh ns] a stumbling block created by the serpent, mixing lies with truth, in order to trick the masses into believing in more than one god; the idea of coexist.
04. Revelation 4:6
05. [ih-man-yoo-uhl-iz-uhm] the doctrinal teaching of realism, realizing that the teachings of Jesus Christ are the only way of life and true words of the Creator; differentiated from Religions, a stumbling block from the serpent.

cial literary term. A sea of glass like unto crystal represents the earth and what's to come in the future; while serpent the imitator provides his followers with a crystal ball. As the four beasts verbalize Holy, holy, holy, Lord God Almighty, which was, and is, and is to come; and later bow before to worship the Lamb worthy of opening the seven seals, the beasts come in agreement that the Father, the Son, and the Holy Spirit are one: Godhead. Entering into <u>One Thousand Two Hundred and Sixty Days</u>: the beast out of the sea will soon come to the realization that prophecies provided by "Allah God Almighty" beguiled from the crystal ball, differentiated from the sea of glass.

The first beast was like a lion;†[06] emblematic of the Antichrist, who attempts to mimic the Lion of Judah: worshipped by many as the Messiah. "Come and see,"†[07] stated the first beast foreboding its distinct identity, symbolically represented on earth as the Apocalyptic White Horse: the Antichrist—crowned king of kings on earth by the nations—hacks on the white horse, after stealing an arrow from Columbia's Secret Signet; and he went forth conquering, and to conquer.

The second beast was like a calf;†[08] emblematic of Religions—any stumbling block, as the serpent provides an alternative god to worship—a Golden Calf:†[09] drawing attention and Jehovah-images away from God Almighty. "Come and See,"†[10] stated the second beast foreboding its distinct identity, symbolically represented on earth as the Apocalyptic Red Horse: a man named Religions wearing a coexist pendant waving a great sword, hacks on the red horse to war against Emmanuelists, and later the religions in which he represents will battle one another; taking peace from the earth.

---

06. Revelation 4:7
07. Relevation 6:1
08. Revelation 4:7
09. Exodus 32:2-4
10. Revelation 6:3

The third beast had a face as a man;†[11] emblematic of mammon as humans worship dead presidents. "Come and See,"†[12] stated the third beast foreboding its distinct identity, symbolically represented on earth as the Apocalyptic Black Horse: the man hacking on the black horse exemplifies the kings of the nations around the world, despairingly attempting to manage their food insufficiency due to their financial collapse via a pair of balances. Post Script: How blessed would be the man who worshipped God and not mammon?

The fourth beast was like a flying eagle;†[13] emblematic of New Babylon as the Great Prostitute convinced the New World to accept the Antichrist as "Messiah": promoting to restore "peace and safety" across the globe. "Come and See,"†[14] stated the fourth beast foreboding its distinct identity, symbolically represented on earth as the Apocalyptic Pale Horse: the man hacking on the pale horse was called Death, and Hell followed with him; And power was giving unto New Babylon to kill with religious wars, food insufficiency, and with death: by way of the serpent out of the bottomless pit as he embodies the Antichrist; destined for fire and brimstone.

One Thousand Two Hundred and Sixty Days

To honor the Olive Sisters death Kirtana and the Devotees celebrated life at the third temple in Jerusalem, accompanied by twelve thousand Emmanuelists. Belial received word of the me-

---

11. Revelation 4:7
12. Revelation 6:5
13. Revelation 4:7
14. Revelation 6:7

morialization transpiring at Jerusalem's new temple and took great interest in crashing the party. Espy the White and Red Apocalyptic Horse as Belial and the Muslim Brotherhood/the Abeyance attempted the trample the third temple of the Lord, hindered by Kirtana and the ten remaining Devotees, predisposed to struggle against Belial's army. The dead in Christ will raise first, demonstrated Belial, conquering Kirtana and the ten remaining Devotees.

In the midst of the battle between the Devotees and Belial, Yeshua stood exalted before the throne of the temple to speak to the twelve thousand Emmanuelists. "As I previously stated, no one will trample this Holy ground without struggle, therefore, come up hither, the time is near for the trumpets to sound," Yeshua spoke in a Many Oceans Dialect, however Belial and the Abeyance heard Yeshua's "Come up hither" in a Thundering Accent; suddenly the twelve thousand Emmanuelists raptured into the heavens for Belial and the Abeyance to witness.

After witnessing Yeshua and the Emmanuelists enter the heavens, Belial spoke on Yeshua's Holy pulpit, and as a second Inauguration before the world proclaimed to be the Lord. "My Holy temple is constructed. Behold, behold, aforementioned and omnipresent I am before thee. I have exalted my throne above the stars of God, I sit upon the mount of the congregation; I am with a capitalized L, the Lord of Lords; forthwith, every specimen bow before me, or with your braincase pay the repercussions. Allah God Almighty has turned his face on the world, and entrusted I to create commandment," Belial spoke with a Lion's Accent, as an Apocalyptic Pale Horse appeared in the spiritual world, revealing the future through a sea of glass mingled with religious wars, food insufficiency, and death seen throughout the world. "Come all, come bow before ..." Abruptly déjà vu entered Belial's introspection of the Olive sisters ascend into heaven, while a great earthquake trembled Mother Earth's axis.†[15]

---

15. Revelation 6:12

"How long, O Lord, holy and true, dost thou not judge and avenge our blood on them that dwell on the earth?" quoted Kirtana and the ten Devotees while accompanying the Olive sisters in the third heaven as the earth trembled: and white robes were given to Kirtana, the ten Devotees and twelve thousand Emmanuelists—undifferentiated from the robes currently attired by the Olive sisters. Suddenly the sun became black as sackcloth of hair and the moon became as blood.†[16]

Herculean fright fell upon Belial as he remembered the Olive sisters' raiment now featured in the sun's emergence from a thunderhead. Suddenly every contributing factor of the chessboard—kings of the earth, great men, rich men, chief captains, mighty men, bondman, and free man—hid themselves within the Area Fifty One's of the earth, and pleaded with the Areas' geographic roofing saying, "Hide us from Lord Yeshua's wrath, son of our Creator; His wrath is upon us."†[17]

Thereupon appeared four angels on the four corners of the earth,†[18] holding the four winds of the earth—undifferentiated from the Prince of the Power of Air, forbearingly waiting on orders from the Prince of Peace to plague the earth and sea: orders conveyed by the turning of Yeshua's face from earth. An angel having the seal of the living God cried to the four apocalyptic angels, "Hurt not the earth, neither the sea, nor the trees, till we have sealed the servants of our God in their foreheads." Subsequently Emmanuelists from the Twelve Tribes of Israel across the earth raptured into the third heaven: twelve thousand from tribe Juda, Reuben, Gad, Aser, Nepthalim, Manasses, Simeon, Levi, Issachar, Zabulon, Joseph, and Benjamin: together equaling one hundred forty four thousand. The Twelve Tribes of Israel consists of all races, six tribes plus six additional tribes equaling the human race, and the human race equaling

16. Revelation 6:12
17. Revelation 6:15-17
18. Revelation 7:1-17

one blood.†[19]

Once in the third heaven one hundred forty four thousand Emmanuelists were arrayed in white robes, made white by the blood of Lamb Yeshua. While standing before the throne of God the Emmanuelists served Yeshua day and night in his temple as He dwelled among them. Hunger and thirst metamorphosed into myth, alike, sunlight producing heat also metamorphosed into myth; whereas the glory of the Lamb provided light, nourishment, and living fountains of waters: in addition the Father wiped away all tears from their eyes.†[20] However the earth below would experience the turning of God's face: in which is His grace and providence.

"I will not be amongst you long" recalled the Jehovah-images personally warned by Yeshua to turn from their sinful ways before the expiration of the acceptable year of the Lord, as apocalyptic trumpets sound. Six apocalyptic trumpets equaled the number of man, and the plagues man must acquiesce due to their participation in the Great Prostitute's fornications: espy Angel Heptad and the Six Angel Band, orchestrating bitter sounds with the application of apocalyptic trumpets.

Angel Pioneer†[21] trumpeted hail and fire on earth mingled with blood, resulting in the rapid oxidation of a third of all green grass. As the Contributors of the Chessboard remained sheltered until the passing of apocalyptic weather conditions, the plebeian nonbelievers in Yeshua desperately waited on those attired in black and white to mount their black horses and come to their aids. An Apocalyptic Pale Horse revealed plebeian nonbelievers commenting suicide due to a loss of faith in their elected Messiah. While others bowed down to worship Belial's statue, searching for a supernatural miracle.

---

19. Revelation 7:1–8
20. Revelation 7:14–17
21. Revelation 8:7

Angel Succeeding†[22] trumpeted an asteroid with the proportions of a great mountain burning with fire into the sea—unlike asteroids in the past, thwarted by the Lord on many occasions—substantiated through Jeremiah Fifty-One:Twenty-Five. Thereupon a third of the seafood and boat supply across the world was destroyed, and the sea metamorphosed into hemoglobin from the sea creatures. A sea of glass mingled with black and white horses prophesies the kings of the earth entrenching a Great Plan to regulate a New World Order. "The nations of the earth must unite to survive," quoted the man hacking on the white horse, while the remaining kings of the earth reported to the rider of the white horse the condition of their agriculture and aquaculture in result of the apocalyptic weather conditions.

Angel Tertiary†[23] trumpeted a great star from heaven, less discreet than the great mountain: burning as it were a lamp, and it fell upon the third part of the rivers, and upon the fountains of waters; and as Wormwood sounded from the Mouthpiece through the Bell, a third part of the water became toxicant. A sea of glass mingled with black and white horses prophesies water supply would be an addition to agriculture and aquaculture, adding potable, contributing to the Great Plan.

Angel Quartern†[24] trumpeted across the earth a deprivation of light from Day and Night: as the sun was smitten, and a third part of the moon, and a third part of the stars darkened. Id est, Angel Quartern trumpeted the ushering in of an Apocalyptic White Horse embodied with the serpent nom de guerre Great Dragon, sounding a portraiture of the Prince of Darkness: The light remaining is by reason of the Emmanuelists who were excluded from the rapture to suffer a short tribulation; some patiently wait for Angel Heptad's performance, while others lose faith. Woe, woe, woe, to the nonbelieving inhibiters

22. Revelation 8:8
23. Revelation 8:10-11
24. Revelation 8:12-13

of the earth by reason of Angel Quintan and Angel Hexad who have not sounded their trumpets; and Angel Heptad—lead vocalist—who as of yet has not sounded her Great Voices from heaven.

Angel Quintan†[25] trumpeted the infestation of a locust never scrutinize heretofore by an earthly being, but only by those who have fallen into the bottomless pit. Just as Belial retreated his geographic roofing, he opened the gate to the bottomless pit per the keys released to him by Yeshua before His departure to the Wedding/Great Supper. Following the opening of the bottomless pit, surrounding areas perceived a fumistratus†[26] cloud—merged with locusts—forming from the earth's core; spiritually darkening the atmosphere and physically blocking sunlight.

In addition to the Abeyance, Belial—the environmentalist—was deemed king over the fairytalic†[27] locusts via the Great Dragon; and ordered the locusts not to hurt the grass, neither any green thing, neither any tree; but only those that have not the seal of God in their foreheads. The strength—or tormenting capability—of the locusts paralleled a soldier in the Abeyance: nom de guerre the Scorpions: nom de guerre the Fiery Serpents under the Old Serpent: nom de guerre the Legion White Horses under the Apocalyptic White Horse; and like soldiers of the Abeyance the locust were like unto the Legion White Horses prepared unto battle, yet, unlike the Abeyance the locusts wore crowns like gold indicating Belial only had authority over them due to the Lord's turning of His face from the earth.

Assuming the semblance of humans and four legged beast, the locusts faces were as the faces of men, and their hair as the hair of women; teeth twinning those of a lion. Flying

---

25. Revelation 9:1-12
26. [fyoo-mi-strey-tuhs] a cloud formed by an abundance of smoke, paralleling the characteristics of a stratus.
27. [fair-ee-tah-lik] having the characteristics of a being or object in a fairytale.

with breastplates like the iron breastplate of righteousness, their wings produced a sound resembling the chariots of many horses running into battle against the unrighteous. Tails like unto scorpions, sting in their tails, their torment caused men to seek death, but death was not found. Belial's power over the locust lasted five months; during these five months umpteen Belialians†[28] ascertained Belial's nefarious acts—hidden by his charm—and ran to the churches that were left behind, showering them with riches, in order to find grace with the Lord.

Angel Hexad†[29] trumpeted the four angels, symbolically sitting on the four corners of the earth by reason of the effects that the angels will have on the entire earth, previously bound in the great river Euphrates: now loose due to the turning of Yeshua's face from earth, ordered by the Prince of the Power of Air—the environmentalist—to not hurt the grass, neither any green thing, neither any tree, but to slay a third part of men on earth. The four angels and the four beast worshipping Godhead are homologous: angel one emblematizes God's wrath for the worship of devils—plagues to be carried out by the Apocalyptic White Horse; angel two emblematizes God's wrath for the worship of idols of gold, and silver, and brass, and stone, and wood—plagues to be carried out by the Apocalyptic Red Horse; angel three emblematizes God's wrath for the worship of mammon, causing murder, creating sorceries and thefts—plagues to be carried out by the Apocalyptic Black Horse; angel four emblematizes God's wrath for the worship of the Great Prostitute, committing fornication—plagues to be carried out by the Apocalyptic Pale Horse.

Four Apocalyptic Horses fulfill Georgia Guidestones, and the number of horsemen was two hundred thousand: each horseman sounding a distinctive gallop. The horses were allied

---

28. [bee-lee-uhl-ee-uhn] a devotee or extreme supporter of Belial; a sheep; designated for lake of fire and brimstone.
29. Revelation 9:13-20

with the locusts, contrived through their resemblance; however the horses lacked a golden crown replaced by the crown of a serpent,†³⁰ indicating that of them, Belial had complete control: Tails like unto scorpions, sting in their tails, heads as the heads of lions described them, because they are the Legion White Horses; "You belong to us," quoted the horses by way of fire and smoke and brimstone, killing another third of Belialians from the earth, as Belial—the environmentalist—maintained humanity under five hundred million, in "perpetual" balance with nature.

Following the performance by the Six Angel Band, the remaining Belialians notwithstanding refused to repent for their worship of devils, and idols of gold, and silver, and brass, and stone, and of wood; neither for their murders, sorcery, fornication, and thefts: therefore for the Belialians, lead vocalist Angel Heptad's performance will be trumpeted like Woe opposed to Blessing.

A continuance of the sixth Woe is the continuance of Angel Hexad's performance, now trumpeting the Mighty Angel†³¹ of No Further Adjournment, limiting the time leading to Earth Beast and Sea Beast's case and judgment, as Mighty Angel held a little book titled "Tribulation of the Guilty Pleasurers" setting his right foot upon the sea and his left foot on the earth. Mighty Angel came down clothed with a cloud: and a rainbow was upon his head, and his face was as it were the sun, and his feet as pillars of fire; a representation of Yeshua's second coming in the clouds: standing on mount Sion shepherding one hundred forty four thousand Emmanuelists, with the Father's name written in their foreheads; to battle the army commanded by Belial nom de guerre Commander in Chief nom de

---

30. Revelation 9:17-19 - heads like lions (heads of the horses were as the heads of lions); and crowns like a serpent (for their tails were like unto serpents, and had heads).
31. Revelation 10:1-11

guerre Sea Beast, supported by Earth Beast.

Mighty Angel†[32] then cried with a loud voice, and seven thunders uttered their voices, and the things not written in Revelation Ten:Four was the seven vials of wrath: seven thunders representing Yeshua's Thundering Accent. In pursuit, one of Pastor Booker's Geotic-Virtues christened Arthur Bishop dreamed a heavenly dream. In the dream, Pastor Booker swallowed the little book titled "Tribulation of the Guilty Pleasurers," and in his mouth it was sweet as honey but bitter in the belly: indicating that sin is pleasurable to the flesh but harmful to the soul nom de guerre the temple, and in the little book contained those who were still on earth, possessing little time to make amends with God and repent for their sins. With this heavenly dream, Arthur Bishop was sent to prophesy before many peoples, and nations, and tongues, and kings.

Angel Heptad†[33] trumpeted and sung a song of great voices in heaven, saying, the kingdoms of this world are becoming the kingdoms of our Lord, and of his Christ; and he shall reign for ever and ever: Traveling the earth by way of the Largesse, Arthur Bishop continued the teachings of the Olive sisters and Yana, preaching that there are more plagues to come and warning those who are still stumbling by a stumbling block to walk from darkness towards the Light. The nations of the world pigeonholed Arthur Bishop's teaching and cared not to hear about the Lord's forthcoming wrath, not yet prepared to die to their old selves and live for Christ.

The Lord conveyed dreams into the minds of the Emmanuelists who were left behind in order to administer hope, and as conformation that the dreams were of the Lord He made it a point for the Emmanuelists to connect with one another via an identical vision, as one invading their conversation would hear them say: And I looked, and, lo, Yeshua stand on the mount

32. Revelation: 10:1-4
33. Revelation 11:15-18

Sion, and with Him the one hundred forty four thousand Emmanuelist in which raptured into heaven from the four winds, and since the Lord promised Candlestick Philadelphia that He would keep them from the hour†[34] of temptation, the four angels released the four winds before their prepared hour, and day, and month, and year. The Emmanuelists were all arrayed in white robes, made white by the blood of Lamb Yeshua; and they sung a new song before the throne, and before the four beasts, and the elders: and no man could learn that song but the one hundred forty four thousand Emmanuelists that were redeemed from the earth.†[35]

Six churches of Asia continued to exist after the rapture of Kirtana, the Devotees, twelve thousand Emmanuelists, and one hundred forty four thousand Emmanuelists: Candlestick Ephesus, Candlestick Smyrna, Candlestick Pergamos, Candlestick Thyatira, Candlestick Sardis, and Candlestick Laodicea. Every church of Asia understood their personality, and furthermore understood why they were left to suffer an abbreviated tribulation. Angel Heptad continued to trumpet as the tempted but not yet forsaken churches obtained the only source of the Holy Spirit via their Candlesticks: in a world darkened by the bottomless pit, and darkened by the turning of the Lord's face.

All <u>One Thousand Two Hundred and Sixty Days</u>: prophetically prophecies became reality, as Belial's face transforms into the likeness of that old serpent, called the Devil, and Satan. In a world physically controlled by the serpent, devastation metamorphosed into the new good, and preservation metamorphosed into the new bad, by means of the Do Not Judge Me Spirit. Fully schemed into existence, the New World limits all guns to the Abeyance; however murder was still in existence, and when a murder occurred the killer quoted, "Do not judge me" and his case was dismissed. Although preservation was

---

34. Revelation 3:10
35. Revelation 14:1-5

nearly extinct, a new breed of pale horses also came into existence, as Belial kept the world carefree through the use of the Radio-frequency Identification Mark: Belialians can hear Belial state, "Continue to believe in me, and I can bless your chip at any time."

Appertaining to the church and associated with the Do Not Judge Me Spirit, a preacher warning homosexual infernatists about the dangers of dwelling in the lake of fire and brimstone at the second death could be charged with a felony, by vindication of Executive Order - No Discrimination. Inspired by the Do Not Judge Me Spirit supporting LGBTs, the executive order also contained political nomenclature banning discrimination against murderers, whoremongers, sorcerers, idolaters, believers of Religions, or any person characterized by an abomination: and due to Executive Order - No Discrimination the Contributors of the Chessboard were not judged by Belialians for their participation in Nine/Eleven, or other crimes in which they used a scapegoat, but Belialians treated those who revealed the Light like unto criminals.

However Prophets and Emmanuelists—those like Arthur Bishop—were not concerned about being charged with a felony, and continued to warn infernatists to turn towards the Light before Yeshua departed the sky: in response, some infernatist were products of Yana's teachings and became born again; Belialians either gave rewards unto the Prophets and Emmanuelists as an attempt to find favor by God, were unwilling to totally follow His teachings, or remained totally dependent upon Belial's false sense of hope because he embraced—or was not judgmental to—their soulinjurious lifestyles.

After several appearances in which Belial declined to speak but was eager to be seen by the masses in order to be worshipped, he finally spoke before the United Nations, introducing himself as the president of the world:

"America: the red, the white, the blue; let us not morn in

behalf of her death, for she is revived, as I, joined in holy matrimony with all nations of the world. Americans, let us not be egotistical but embraceable; North America is America, South America is America, Africa is America, Antarctica is America, Europe is America, Asia is America, Australia is America: mutatis mutandis. Make no mistake. America remains, meritorious. Nonetheless, one voiced nation becomes all powerful with many. What was made in America or made in China is now made in the New World, forming a world economy. With Israel, let us make amity, and sign a peace treaty; for it is not wise to war against our Heavenly Father's first born. Rumors are evolving that the Lord has taken His bride, and this explains the mysterious disappearance of numerous of our loved ones; my fellow humans a wedding in the sky is highly unscientific and unbiblical, our nations joining as a New World on earth is what the bible refers to, for your Lord is present, therefore let us embrace a world religion. Yes we have shared quondam differences, notwithstanding, we as living beings are forthwith in a war against vitality, and we must officially establish peace and security. Follow me in an, infrangible, pilgrimage towards world peace. O Father in heaven; bless this New World," Belial addressed, in a Dragon Lion Accent.

Years betide after Belial's speech on world unity, as the world's atmosphere continued to darken by spirit with the feeling of a false peace. The only light shined from the six Candlesticks, and even the six Candlesticks became one, holding the personality of Candlestick Philadelphia. The Candlestick's who disregarded the warning by the Prophets, and Emmanuelists, and Arthur Bishops, their candlesticks could not stand, and were blown out from the Prince of the Power of Air's rule: devastated by the tribulation. Woe, woe, woe, it is now time for the Lord's last warning; the seven vials of wrath, concluding what Angel Heptad and the Six Angel Band entrenched.

Espy Phial Moiety, a rap group sampling Angel Heptad

and the Six Angel Band's song "Great and Marvelous Are Thy Works, Lord God Almighty." The rap group consists of seven angels creating their own musical category called Text Music. Each of Phial Moiety's members contributed their hottest single for the completion of their first Long-playing record nom de plume LP, titled The Lord's Wrath:

Intro: And I looked, and behold a white cloud, and upon the cloud one sat: His body was like the beryl, and his face as the appearance of lightning, and his eyes as lamps of fire, and his arms and his feet like in colour to polished brass, and the voice of his words like the voice of a multitude.†[36] And it was seen from a sea of glass mingled with ballets electing Yeshua after the great winepress of the wrath of God—making all things new; fire mingled with the sea of glass revealed the beast in his fiery kingdom, after the dwellers on earth got victory over the beast, and over his image, and over his mark, over the number of his name.†[37]

Track One - Vial of Wrath Un: "As the Lord speaks in a Thundering Accent, woe to those who have accepted the mark of the beast and have worshipped the beast's image," Angel One raps in his song's hook. Suddenly a grievous sore came upon those with the RFID chip, a sore clearly seen in the forehead or the right hand after the chip malfunctioned: due to the falling of hail and fire; a mingling of blood was due to the grievous sore from the chip's malfunction.†[38]

Track Two - Vial of Wrath Deux: "As the Lord speaks in a Thundering Accent, every living soul in the sea died, and blood saturated the sea," Angel Two raps in his song's hook. Suddenly a greater asteroid mountain burning with fire expunges every living sea creature. An Apocalyptic Black Horse travels the globe, as nations look towards Belial to supernaturally solve a

36. Daniel 10:6
37. Revelation 15:2-4
38. Revelation 16:2

worsened aquaculture insufficiency.†[39]

Track Three - Vial of Wrath Trois Ft. Angel Anonymous: "The Lord has spoken in his Thundering Accent ('can your bottled drinks stand,' echoes in a soft woman's voice from the right speaker to the left), Thou art righteous, O Lord, which art, and wast, and shalt be, because thou hast judged thus. For they have shed the blood of saints and prophets, and thou hast given them blood to drink; for they are worthy,"†[40] Angel Three raps in his verse.

"Even so, Lord God Almighty, true and righteous are thy judgments," sings Angel Anonymous following Angel Three's verse. As Angel Three's engineer mixes the vocals, nations across the globe report their deprivation of water supply to Belial: An Apocalyptic Black Horse travels the globe, as nations look towards Belial to supernaturally solve a worsened water insufficiency.

Track Four - Vial of Wrath Quatre: "As the Lord speaks in a Thundering Accent, the sun's smite sends solar flares following the sprinkling of particles onto earth, causing record breaking temperatures, scorching the inhibitors on earth with heat,"†[41] Angel Four raps in his verse following the hook. "How could you blaspheme God and not repent? How could you blaspheme God and not repent. How could you blaspheme God and not repent? How could you (echo)…not give him glory?" After the hook there was a manifestation of the single Vial of Wrath Quatre, as the inhibitors on earth realized that the plagues were cause by the wrath of God Almighty.

Track Five - Vial of Wrath Cinq: Vial of Wrath Quatre fades into Vial of Wrath Cinq and there was a sense of darkness as the Lord speaks in a Thundering Accent. "You thought you were the king of them, silly you, you hold no power over

---

39. Revelation 16:3
40. Revelation 16:4
41. Revelation 16:8-9

Him. Here's a taste of your medicine, you think you god, take a plague—this is heaven sent," Angel Five raps in his verse, and what was not clear in the song becomes clear as day to Sea Beast: The scorpions first controlled by Belial are presently controlled by their true King, presently tormenting Belial and his administration. Nevertheless instead of repenting for their deeds, Belial and his administration blasphemed God of heaven because of their pains and sores.†[42]

Track Six - Vial of Wrath Six: "As the Lord speaks in a Thundering Accent, the great river Euphrates dried up to make a way for the Legion White Horses," Angel Six quotes in his single's chorus. Immediately Belial and the Pope work miracles via the spirits of devils to stage an alien evasion. Unclean spirits like frogs reveal a fallacious form of persuasion, as Belial—embodied by the Great Dragon—and the Pope, pull Belialians and citizens of the New World in by way of a toad's tongue, gathering the armies of the world to fight against the aliens, knowing the "invasion" would actually consist of Yeshua and the armies of heaven:†[43]

"A blitzkrieg against the inhabitants of the earth has been declared. The authenticity that we are not companionless in this universe is indisputable, and lamentably through several instances of communication it is understood that our companions desire to inhabit earth absent of our dwelling. What is even more burdensome is the palpability that Israel has erewhile stipulated with our future invaders an alliance. Incontestably we are cognizant of the plagues that have pulverized us all; these plagues are a direct result of the unhesitatingly approaching invasion. Contrary to our peace treaty, counteroffensive is not only necessary but an obligation. Make no mistake, peace is our concupiscence, and after this battle peace will immediately supervene; but in order to perpetuate peace we must not accept

---

42. Revelation 16:10-11
43. Revelation 16:12-14

vanquishment. Nations of the world let us eradicate our aggressors for our freedom, and officially establish indivisibility," Belial bespeaks in a Lion Accent while embodied by the Great Dragon, convincing the world to fight against God Almighty, following in moderation a toad's tongue by the Pope.

"Let us embrace Islam's Messiah: Mahdi: Belial Fulgurite [foo l-grit] as our Christ while we unite all religions into one. I am positive that he will lead our world into peace after the fight for our freedom against our invaders. I have a word from the Most High; He stated that He would guide us through this encroachment, so do not fear: Fearfulness does not know Faith. Call your loved ones because an escape from death is not promised: tell them that you love them and encourage them with kind words. This nightmare will soon be over. God Bless the New World," the Pope bespeaks in a Dragon Accent.

Then Mighty Angel took up a stone—tied to a statue like unto the Statue of Freedom—like a great millstone, and casted it in the sea.†⁴⁴ "Thus with violence shall that great city New Babylon be thrown down, and shall be found no more at all," said Mighty Angel; and what manifests in the spiritual, manifests in the physical.

Track Seven - Vial of Wrath Sept Ft. Angel Heptad: "There came a great voice out of the temple of heaven as the Lord speaks in a Thundering Accent, from the throne, saying, "It is done." And there were lightings from His Accent, and there was a great earthquake, such as was not since men were upon the earth, so mighty an earthquake, and so great,"†⁴⁵ Angel seven quotes in his verse leading into the chorus, and there were voices singing alone with Angel Heptad: "We give thee thanks, O Lord God Almighty, which art, and wast, and art to come. Because thou hast taken to thee thy great power, and hast reigned; hast taken to thee thy great power, and hast reigned."

---

44. Revelation 18:21
45. Revelation 16:17-18

After Angel Heptad sung on the chorus, a glass mingled with the prophets, and to the Emmanuelists, and them that fear Thy name, small and great received their rewards from Yeshua.

Following the Long-playing record titled The Lords Wrath, the great city was divided into three parts due to the mighty earthquake, and the cities of the nations fell: and great Babylon came in remembrance before God, to give unto her the cup of the wine of the fierceness of His wrath: The Statue of Freedom's illumination extinguishes as the cup of wine over-flows causing every island to flee, dividing while destroying the Assembled States, and the mountains could not be found. And there fell upon men a great hail out of heaven, every hail stone the weight of gold money talents—representing the Great Prostitutes fornications, and men blasphemed God because of the plague of the hail.†⁴⁶

Pope of the Chessboard: king of the world: False Proph-et: Earth Beast moves diagonally on earth's chessboard while Horse of the Chessboard: President of Columbia: Sea Beast slithers forward in an L shape to take Earth Beast's position with a checkmate; before becoming king of the world, Belial de-throned kings who were uncooperative in regards to the Great Plan, via americide, replacing the kings with members of his Brotherhood, paving the way for a ten sovereign international kingdom. These shall make war with the Lamb, and the Lamb shall overcome them: for he is Lord of lords, and King of kings: and they that are with Him are called, and chosen, and faith-ful:†⁴⁷

In strong dislike of the Pope's original religious views and costumes, the Muslim Brotherhood convinces Belial to or-der the Pope to change the Vatican's purple and scarlet colored garments to the Sacred Color of Islam: In reference to Leviticus Twenty-One:Nine through Ten, in the eyes of the faithful the

46. Revelation 16:19-21
47. Revelation 17:12-14

Pope was no longer high priest because he was no longer in his consecrated garment, and the Pope's Great Whore profaned her Father: she was burnt with fire; moreover the Great Whore's flesh was eaten: as Belial sacrifices the Vatican to the serpent; for God hath put in their hearts to fulfill his will, and to agree, and give their kingdom unto the beast, until the words of God shall be fulfilled.†[48]

Replaying Vial of Wrath Sept Ft. Angel Heptad in order to fully comprehend the single's libretto, the Great Prostitute nom de plume the Statue of Freedom: a representation of the Great Whore: dwelling in Big Apple's sea to also represent the Assembled States, asphyxiates in the sea, and the mountains on her crown—representing every Continental Head—could not be found. Forty-Three islands accompany the Great Prostitute's destruction as the mighty earthquake divides Big Apple into three parts causing the islands to flee. While the east coast of New Babylon suffered the effects of the mighty earthquake, the west coast continued to suffer the effects of the Hoover Dam tragedy.

Expanding from the east, and west, and north, and south, a circumloccrate†[49] spiritually encompassed New Babylon: becoming the habitation of devils, foul spirits, and every unclean hateful bird; and the world experienced a falling away due to New Babylon's influence, merchants of the earth are waxed rich through the abundance of her delicacies.†[50] "Come out of her, my people!" quoted Yeshua within the minds of the remaining Emmanuelist who continued to with her unequally yoke, "Be not partakers of her sins, and that ye receive not of her plagues; for her sins have reached unto heaven, and God hath remembered her iniquities." For those who consider mourning, let us

---

48. Revelation 17:15-17
49. [ser-kuhm-loh-kreyt] a spiritual or physical barrier bonding an area, city, or nation.
50. Revelation 18:1-3

remember her highly televised court case.

"Thou shall not kill: Thus how long, O New Babylon, have you shed blood in order to become and remain a preeminent distributor?" asked the Lord, for no one on earth was powerful enough to try her case, but strong is the Lord God who judged her.

"I am the preeminent distributor of slaves from Fifteen Zero One through Eighteen Sixty Five, not including the soldiers killed in war approximately One Hundred Million lives were claimed in order to keep my distribution prosperous," stated New Babylon; boastfully claiming her history.

"Thou shall not kill: Thus how long, O New Babylon, have you shed blood in order to become and remain a preeminent distributor?" asked the Lord; for no one on earth was powerful enough to try her case, but strong is the Lord God who judged her.

"I am the preeminent distributor of diamonds from Nineteen Sixty One through Present Day, not including the soldiers killed, approximately Four Million lives were claimed in order to keep my distribution prosperous," stated New Babylon; refusing to ban diamond mining.

"Thou shall not kill: Thus how long, O New Babylon, have you shed blood in order to become and remain a preeminent distributor?" asked the Lord; for no one on earth was powerful enough to try her case, but strong is the Lord God who judged her.

"I am the preeminent distributor of Planned Parenthood from Nineteen Sixteen through Present Day, approximately Sixty Million baby lives have been claimed in order to keep my distribution prosperous," stated New Babylon; showing no indication of repentance.

In the middle of court proceedings there was an outburst from many of New Babylon's merchants saying, "Alas, alas, that great city Babylon, that mighty city! For in one hour is thy judgment come."

And the Lord pummels His gavel saying, "Order in the court; I have remembered her iniquities and judgment has come."

"Thou shall not commit adultery, Thou shall not steal, Thou shalt have no other gods before me, and Thou shall not covet: Thus how long, O New Babylon, have you led souls astray in order to become and remain a preeminent distributor?" asked the Lord; for no one on earth was powerful enough to try her case, but strong is the Lord God who judged her.

"I am the preeminent distributor of Unclean Spirits like Frogs Entertainment from the Nineteen Hundred's through Present Day; souls of men are sold worldwide and enter the bottomless pit due to our products, whereas we influentially encourage idolatry and the idol: encourages adultery, causes one to covet their purple nom de plume showy items nom de plume finer things in life like gold, pearls, fine linen, silk, houses furnished with ivory, precious wood, brass, iron and marble; moreover when the impoverished covets it encourages them to steal in order to impersonate their idol. Nonetheless, Unclean Spirits like Frogs Entertainment's greatest accomplishment is mind control; who would know that they have the desire to commit adultery because of the women in our videos, or desire to steal to impersonate our artists, or who would know that we encourage them to worship us or our god? In general, we pull our spectators in like a frog's tongue, with our super-ordinary inventiveness," stated New Babylon; sitting as a queen with no widow: utterly arrogant.

After her testimony, fire fell from the sky and into the circumloccrate encompassing New Babylon, and the smoke released from her burning displayed her judgment. "Alas, alas, that great city, that was clothed in fine linen, and purple, and scarlet, and decked with gold, and precious stones, and pearls!" Quoted the merchants who witnessed the smoke aboard; but for the shipmaster merchants floating close by in the sea, the dust from the smoke entered their upper decks, therefore they casted the dust on their heads, and cried, weeping and wailing, saying, "Alas, alas, that great city, wherein were made rich all that had ships in the sea by reason of her costliness! It seemed like an eternity, but her desolation befell in an hour."†[51]

While the merchants on earth wept and wailed, the heaven and holy apostles and prophets rejoiced over her; for God hath avenged them on her. And no super-ordinary inventiveness was found from Unclean Spirits like Frogs Entertainment; and no craftsman—one that would make a graven image of God, or likeness of anything that is in heaven above, or likeness of anything in the earth beneath, or likeness of anything that is in the water under the earth, of whatsoever craftsman he be, shall be found any more in thee, New Babylon; and the second drowning of a stone like a great millstone could not be performed by Mighty Angel because no more shall thee, New Babylon, be found; and the light of a candle—represented by the Statue of Freedom's prideful raised hand—shall shine no more at all in thee; and the voice of Yeshua and of His bride shall be heard no more at all in thee: for thy merchants were the "gods" of the earth; for by thy sorceries were all nations deceived.

Henceforth, innumerable vociferations amalgamated as one great voice saying "Alleluia; Salvation, and glory, and honor, and power, unto the Lord our God: for true and righteous are his Judgments: for he has judged the Great Whore, which did corrupt the earth with her fornications, and has avenged the blood of his servants at her hand."†[52] And after a second Alleluia vocalized by the great voice, Smoke Signal stated, "Everlasting fumata nera,"†[53] and the merchants were reminded of New Babylon's dark smoke, and they vocalized in one voice saying,

51. Revelation 18:9-19
52. Revelation 19:1-2
53. Revelation 19:3

"Great Whore's smoke resembles that of our Great Prostitute."

Smoke from the Great Whore and the Great Prostitute also resembled an end to the spirit of worshipping false Messiahs, idols, mammon, and New Babylon; as the four and twenty elders and the four beasts fell down and worshipped God that sat on the throne, saying, "Amen; Alleluia."†[54]

"Praise our God, all ye His servants, and ye that fear Him, both small and great. Alleluia: for the Lord God omnipotent reigneth,"†[55] Yeshua responded; with great multitude in His Many Ocean and Thundering Accent.

In reminiscence of Belial's speech the nations of the world were anxious to get revenge against the invaders for Babylon's destruction, turbulently anticipating what was thought to be their inevitable destruction. Patiently but eagerly, Belial, his international army, and the False Prophet invaded Israel; and sojourned near Armageddon nom de plume Megiddo to prepare for the "alien invasion." Then Eagerly showed his evil face and Belial grew impatient, and since Israel is the apple of God's eye, Belial allowed his brotherhood to divide the land saying, "Where is your God, O Israel? Jerusalem is no longer yours." And then Belial ordered the killing of all Emmanuelists in his mind, and betrays them with a kiss:

"All believers in Christ: Be accessible and with I assemble; unassailability, due to your place in the Lord, empowers you to abandon your place of wilderness without faintheartedness. I wish to extent my hospitality to counterbalance my personification of the antichrist, for I am a type of Christ, like Melchizedek, a king of peace. Do I not exemplify a peaceful being from my speeches on unity? Be accessible and with I assemble, for I have prepared a great supper with my brothers in Christ, let us display to the world brotherly love. Come assemble in the third temple," Belial briefly states; attempting to convince the

54. Revelation 19:4
55. Revelation 19:5

remaining Emmanuelists to leave their prepared habitations.

"How long, O Lord, holy and true, dost thou not judge and avenge our blood on them that dwell on the earth?" And it was said to them with the white robes, "It is time." Previously guided by the Lord's voice, the Emmanuelists who obtained Candlestick Philadelphia were not warned that Belial's invitation was a deception, thence familiar with the Lord's providence and grace, comfortableness after decampment and a great supper overtook their perceptions. Thereupon millions of Emmanuelists assembled at the third temple, near that place called Armageddon, to meet Belial at the entrance; however Belial and his army failed to enter.

Due to the unsuccessful attempt to perform a massacre within the third temple, Belial sets up his guillotines on the temple's land; and Belial, the kings of the earth, and their armies proceeded to perform the greatest massacre of Emmanuelists in world's history.†[56] In reference to Revelation Six:Eleven, the raptured Emmanuelists' fellow servants were killed, numbering millions, as Belial and his Abeyance commemorated chanting, "Our god is the only god! Our god is the only god! Peace be to Mahdi! We have conquered the infidels! We have conquered the infidels!"

Suddenly Belial receives a vision from the Lord: Kirtana, the twelve devotees, twelve thousand Emmanuelists, one hundred forty four thousand raptured Emmanuelists, Emmanuelists that were murdered by his guillotine massacre, among others, were arrayed in fine linen, clean and white—for the fine linen represented the righteousness of the Emmanuelists; thereafter Belial receives a vision of Melchizedek†[57] and Pastor Booker on earth:

"Let us be glad and rejoice, and give honour to him: for the marriage of the Lamb is come, and his wife hath made her-

---

56. Revelation 20:4
57. Hebrews 7:1-20 - the Archangel holding the Word of God Almighty.

self ready. Blessed are they which are called unto the marriage supper of the Lamb. These are the true saying of God," quoted Melchizedek; and Pastor Booker fell at his feet to worship him. "See thou do it not: I am thy fellow-servant, and of thy brethren that have the testimony of Jesus: worship God: for the testimony of Jesus is the spirit of prophecy,"†[58] ended Melchizedek to Pastor Booker; vividly contemplated within Belial's vision.

Then Belial recovered from his vision with a refusal to repent attitude, and heaven opened straightaway. Thereupon, a halo separated the clouds and blue sky. Within the halo appeared a white light, and the white light rays beamed over the halo's circumference, dimming the sun. In the mist of the white light the nose of the white horse emerged, and when the white horse was conclusively revealed it was like unto a Pegasus. He that sat upon the horse was called Faithful and True, and in righteousness He doth judge and make war. His eyes were as a flame of fire, and on His head were many crowns; and He had a name written, that no man knew, but He Himself. And He was clothed with a vesture dipped in blood: and His name is called The Word of God.†[59]

The halo's diameter up surged in size as the armies which were in heaven followed Yeshua, and the armies that followed also sat upon white horses, clothed in fine linen, white and clean.†[60] Out of Yeshua's mouth gives forth a Sharp Sword Accent, that with it He should smite the nations: and He shall rule them with a rod of iron: and He treadeth the winepress of the fierceness and wrath of Almighty God. And He hath on His vesture and on His thigh a name written, KING OF KINGS, AND LORD OF LORDS.†[61]

When Belial noticed white light rays beam over the halo's

58. Revelation 19:9-10
59. Revelation 19:11-12
60. Revelation 19:14
61. Revelation 19:15-16

circumference, he took the glorious vision of Yeshua's coming as a threat, and called for an Air Defense Warning Red. Like a domino effect a seraph stood in the sun, and with the fowls that fly in the midst of heaven, called for the great supper of the great God.†⁶² Following the Air Defense Warning Red the ten kings from the New World gathered their armies on pale horses, blasphemously equipped with Bushmasters labeled Saturday Night Special—with the intentions of mocking the Sabbath, and stood their ground, as Yeshua and His army touched the terrain on the gathered armies' opposition to make war. While New World vultures circled the battle, the Emmanuelists clothed in fine linen, equipped with iron rods nom de plume mighty swords, began to rule over the nations; righteously worthy to provide flesh for the New World vultures.

Betwixt and between the battle Belial and the False Prophet scrambled to escape, cautious of the Emmanuelists swords; but terrified of Yeshua: the King of kings, and His Sharp Sword Accent. Unable to eschew His Sharp Doubled Edged Sword, the avoidance of adjudication was not a possibility and the both of them were forced to bow before Yeshua while the battle progressed. Those who watched the battle from abroad bowed on their knees, and all nations and all tongues and all human beings confessed that Jesus Christ was Lord; as the loins of every jungle roared.

Who could bear a sword to a gun fight and triumph? (Those not of the world, but have become transcendental through the blood of Yeshua; becoming eternal beings). No weapon that is formed against thee shall prosper; and every tongue that shall rise against thee in judgment thou shall condemn. This is the heritage of the servants of the Lord, and their righteousness is of me, saith the Lord.†⁶³ And like Yeshua the Word came to life: Iron rods or swords dismantle bullet vessels formed by gun pot-

---

62. Revelation 19:17
63. Isaiah 54:17

ters, and soldiers from the Abeyance, the kings of the earth, and their armies are broken to shivers alike; all those judged without due process—sentenced to death due to their faithfulness—were redeemed by the coming of the Lord; however in regards to their opposition: conquered, souls swallowed, the Abeyance, kings of the earth, and their armies settle into their millennium extended home, for the servants of the Lord earned their heritage and ruled the nations, righteousness shimmering owing to their clean and white fine linen.†[64]

Squawks flooded the breeze and blood flooded the terrain as the flesh of the bottomless pitted souls were eaten by the New World vultures. All those from across the globe who took the mark of the beast fell out of their genuflection, worshipping Yeshua, and onto their stomachs in result of cardiac arrest: which was their judgment, conveyed from Yeshua's Sharp Sword Accent; after their souls entered the bottomless pit, their flesh was eaten by the New World vultures alike: all Contributors of the Chessboard, all men both free and bold, both small and great.†[65]

Anon, the lake of fire burning with brimstone was revealed, the Dead Sea, while Yeshua confronted Belial and the False Prophet; as they recovered from their unwanted bow to stand with refusal to repent arrogance, immediately Belial's boldness metamorphosed in trepidation, and the False Prophet's boldness into a slight feeling of repentance only due to his trepidation. "I realize that Satan has played a major role in your executive decisions, but to you I have provided discernment, to distinguish Satan's voice from mine. In return you have followed the Dragon and ignored any offers of repentance, and have angered the Lord God who is slow to anger; your judgment has now come. The both of you are not worthy to dwell in the bottomless pit where you will be worshipped for your fornications;

---

64. Revelation 19:19
65. Revelation 19:21

therefore the second death is yours: your desire to truly resurrect as the Messiah is blasphemous before the Lord; therefore you will have no chance, for the lake of fire and brimstone is where you both will spend your days: forever and ever," stated Yeshua; in a Thundering Sharp Sword Accent, as He casted†[66] Belial and the False Prophet in the lake of fire burning with brimstone.

Thereupon the Dragon, that old serpent, which is the Devil, and Satan, disembodied Belial; and a seraph came down from heaven, having the key of the bottomless pit and in his hand a great chain, saying, "I bind you Satan, to the bottomless pit for a thousand years. May your mouth be shut, thus no more you can deceive the nations, until your time have expired." And the serpent was casted†[67] to the bottomless pit to serve his thousand years after Jehovah's chastisement, advocated by the seraph.

Post hoc, the New World was figedened†[68] into a New Jerusalem posthaste as Yeshua was elected President nom de guerre Kings of kings nom de guerre Lord of lords nom de guerre Prince of peace, and of the increase of his government and peace there shall be no end. Affixed to Yeshua's right side stood Kirtana Miguel, vice president of Yeshua as promised; safeguarding the Invincible and Neotheoic†[69] Commander In Chief's front by reason of devotedness stood the black belted Olive sisters, ready for any bone of contention; and last but not least the remaining ten Devotees stood in the formation of a cross behind Yeshua as He delivered His Inauguration in the

---

66. Revelation 19:20
67. Revelation 20:1-3
68. [fig-eed-n] to form a dreadful place into a paradise, supernaturally or by means of currency.
69. [nee-oh-thee-oh-ik] Modern; New; Recent; God acknowledging any word of the eight parts of speech, or any combination of words as His own, or as His description; being the Alpha and Omega or creator of the word or combination of words.

third temple:

"You are my most faithful servants and to this I say well done. Think not of your resurrection as a right but a blessing, and cherish your blessing honorably as kings and queens. Think of others before you consider yourself, serving your servants, and your servants will graciously serve. I am your God; let me wash your feet in open conversation, as our small talk develops great righteousness; your willingness to learn is significant for your completeness, for the words of the Father is life; let Him breathe into you the blood of the Lamb and you will receive a new name. As of old, you continue to process freewill; however sin will be to you as unwanted filth, for a day with the Lord is like a thousand years, and love of the flesh you will no longer desire, for your renewed flesh will long after the blood of the Lamb. Your children's children that will live at the time of Gog and Magog will suddenly become bored with My reign, and shall follow Satan and Satan will gather them together to battle; therefore raise them in the way that I will raise you, for while in the presence of the Lord you will know not boredom, but like the days of Adam and Eve that old serpent will convince them otherwise. I am your God, and a thousand years we will reign, and you will be with the Lord forever and forever, shout ALLE-LUIA, and give the Father the highest praise," **Yeshua states in a Many Ocean Accent; and all of His most faithful shouted Alleluia as a commencement to the day of a thousand years.**

An omnipotent kingdom has set its place on the earth. Many gods have proclaimed an everlasting throneship,†[70] and many dynasties have been dethroned; however no dynamism will dethrone the All-powerful; for in accordance with neo-theoicism†[71] He is the Creator of creation, the Creator of sov-

---

70. [throhn-ship] holding the position of an everlasting throne, obtained through inheritance.
71. [nee-oh-thee-oh-ik-kiz-uh m] the belief that the Lord is who He says He is, in reverence to any word or combination of words.

ereignty: Unconquerable, yet Indescribably Undefinable. And by virtue of His grace and mercy the Emmanuelist have become kings and queens under Yeshua's amaranthine throneship. A thousand years Yeshua and His most faithful will rule, a millennium day, and they will restore the physical and spiritual destruction created by the serpent. Let all those who believe celebrate the Advent, and celebrate the absence of darkness with a millennium day: at last the King is among us, Hallelujaaaah, hallelujaaaah, let us celebrate this miraculous millennium day.

Glossary

affiliation-epithet [uh-fil-ee-ey-shuhn-ep-uh-thet] noun : conceding that the meaning of a person, place, or thing's name defines it's character.

all-knowledgeableness [awl-nol-i-juh-buhl-nes] adjective : knowledgeable of all things

americide [uh-mer-i-sahyd] noun : the killing of an American that fight's against Columbia's "original propose." − *reverencing Clause 4*

Belialian [bee-lee-uhl-ee-uhn] noun : a devotee or extreme supporter of Belial; a sheep; designated for lake of fire and brimstone.

BoP [bee-oh-pee] noun : the bottom of the pyramid.

Chief Minders [cheef-mahyn-der] noun : top ranked presidential bodyguard; right hand man

convertee [kuhn-vur-tee] noun : a person who converts to another religion.

corduct [kor-duhkt] verb: to pull on one's heart, usually to lead one to the truth.

circumloccrate [ser-kuhm-loh-kreyt] noun: a spiritual or physical barrier bonding an area, city, or nation.

dayably [dey-ey-blee] adjective : worthy of naming a day after

discerntion [dih-surn-shuhn] noun : to distinguish from the Spirit of Truth; addressing the person in which the information revealed was in regards to, in order to get an conformational replay.

Godlove [goh-duhv] noun : the love in God revealed within another individual, passing that love to others.

gustocarn [guhs-toh-kahrn] noun : luxury or designer cloths preened to please the flesh.

Emmanuelan [ih-man-yoo-uhl-uhn] noun : of, pertaining to, believing in, or belonging to the way-of-life based on the teachings of Jesus Christ: God with us

Emmanuelanity [ih-man-yoo-uhl-an-i-tee] noun : the quality of being an Emmanuelan through beliefs and practices, state of being Emmanuelan.

Emmanuelism [ih-man-yoo-uhl-iz-uhm] noun : the doctrinal teaching of realism, realizing that the teachings of Jesus Christ are the only way of life and true words of the Creator; differentiated from Religions, a stumbling block from the serpent.

Emmanuelist [ih-man-yoo-uhl-list] noun : a person who believes in Jesus Christ: God with us

Eyes-wide-exposed [ahyz-wahyd-ik-spohzd] adjective : spiritual eyes open; in tune with the Spirit of Truth

facwad [fak-wod] 1. verb 2. noun : 1. to make rolls of money 2. cash, funds

fairytalic [fair-ee-tah-lik] adjective : having the characteristics of a being or object in a fairytale.

femme vital [fem-vahyt-l] noun : a beautiful woman inside and out; an exquisite woman physically, one who fears God.

figeden [fig-eed-n] verb: to form a dreadful place into a paradise, supernaturally or by means of currency.

fumistratus [fyoo-mi-strey-tuhs] noun : a cloud formed by an abundance of smoke, paralleling the characteristics of a stratus.

importheous [im-pawr-thee-uh-uhs] adjective : having an significant role in fulfilling a spiritual purpose

incantational [in-kan-tey-shuhn-nl] adjective : of or pertaining to the success of incantation

infernate [in-fur-neyt] verb : *infernatist-noun*, verb : to become a part of hell, in result of being sent to; and or on the path leading to hell by the influence of another.

infernatist [in-fur-ney-tist] noun : a person who advertently or inadvertently believes in the Serpent as their god; by rejecting Jesus Christ, the Creator of existence, as their Lord and Savior.

Jehovah-image [ji-hoh-vuh-im-ij] noun : a human; made in His image. - *reverencing Genesis 1:27*

Jehovah-Gmolah [ji-hoh-vuh-guh-moh-luh] noun : The God of Recompense. - *reverencing Jeremiah 51:6*

Jehovah-Sabaoth [ji-hoh-vuh-sab-ee-oth] noun : the Lord of Host, our Protector

minxist [mingks-ist] noun : a woman who believes in whoredom; a sexually promiscuous female

monsacred [mon-sey-krid] noun : a vision from God given while asleep as a warning or insight.

musa [mu'sa] noun : All Powerful intelligence beyond imagination; perennial genius.

neotheoic [nee-oh-thee-oh-ik] adjective : Modern; New; Recent; God acknowledging any word of the eight parts of speech, or any combination of words as His own, or as His description; being the Alpha and Omega or creator of the word or combination of words.

neotheoicism [nee-oh-thee-oh-ik-kiz-uh m] noun : the belief that the Lord is who He says He is, in reverence to any word or combination of words.

New-Age [noo-eyj] the era of human esprit that are influenced by the New World: the Great Prostitute

New Secular [noo-sek-yuh-ler] noun : the music generation in which mocks the Lord; music made by the chief one's - *rev. Isaiah 14:9*

obsightlessly [awb-sahyt-les-lee] adjective : arriving at a place or location unnoticed; unusually appearing physically, the person that as arrived holds great prominence.

Overtone-zither [oh-ver-tohn-zith-er] interjection : an expression used to indicate to the possible occurrence of a mood change; or indicating that someone's mood changed: originating from the Moodswinger (a twelve string electric zither created by Yuri Landman).

paper-specie [pey-per-spee-shee] noun : a slang word for money.

parishe [par-i-shee] noun : a male member in a local church.

parishess [par-i-shsis] noun : a female member in a local church.

playing the serpent [pley-in-thuh-sur-puhnt] noun : an idiom describing a person who low spirited.

Politician [pol-i-tish-uhn] noun : a person or king who is bostowed with a sovereign office.

pseudo-identity [soo-doh-ahy-den-ti-tee] noun : spuriously pretending to be an individual other than one's birthed being via identification; identity thief.

pseudowitlessly [soo-doh-wit-lis-lee] adjective : feign ignorance; the act of playing dumb

Raising Hands Gesture [rey-zing-handz-jes-cher] noun : raising both hands out, as if one were holding the world.

Religions [ri-lij-uh ns] noun : a stumbling block created by the serpent, mixing lies with truth, in order to trick the masses into believing in more than one god; the idea of coexist.

Rerooter [ri-roo-ter] noun : the Spirit of life, holding the ability to revive that which is deprived of life.

sacrificeable [sak-ruh-fahys-ey-buhl] adjective : *sacrificableness-noun*, adjective : willing to be put forth as a sacrifice to the serpent for the purposes of financial advancement and or acceptance

sensitivism [sen-si-tiv-iz-uhm] noun : the doctrine involved in showing sensitivity, or sympathy towards another's hardship; displaying empathy

self-ordealist [self-awr-deel-ist] noun : a person who has convicted themselves to hell, thinking that God would not forgive their particular sin(s).

snarartist [snair-ahr-tist] noun : a person who sacrificed themselves, to the serpent's snare, in pursuance of professionalism affiliated with one of the preforming arts: music, dance, theater, etc.

soulinjurious [sohl-in-joor-ee-uhs] adjective : baleful, cruel, or damaging, as in effecting or attempting to effect the soul.

straitjacket act [streyt-jak-it-akt] noun -*slang* : the act of displaying strange mannerisms; weird behavior

theosire [thee-uh-sahyuhr] noun: a man who practices sacred paternal care over other person(s); a spiritual father

throneship [throhn-ship] noun: holding the position of an everlasting throne, obtained through inheritance.

unsacrificeable [uhn-sak-ruh-fahys-ey-buhl] adjective : *unsacrificableness-noun*, adjective : unwilling to be put forth as a sacrifice to the serpent; reluctant to bend the truth written in the Holy Scripter for the purposes of an earthly acceptance or advancement.

violin [vahy-uh-lin] verb : to string a person along by trickery; to bamboozle; hoodwink.

withload [with-lohd] verb : to remove from the internet due to government restrictions, or due to restrictions established by the site holder.

worldist [wurl-dist] noun : **1.** an individual of the world, eyes not open to the spiritual world **2.** One who is within the snare of the serpent, participation in the great prostitute's fornication.

yeshuanity [yosh-oo-an-i-tee] noun : having or possessing characteristics of Christ through the Holy Spirit or a personnel encounter.

President

Yeshua